The Murder of Angela Dales

Twenty-One Years Later

David Cariens

High Tide
Publications, Inc.
www.HighTidePublications.com

ISBN: 978-1-945990-91-5

Published by High Tide Publications, Inc.
www.hightidepublications.com

Thank you for purchasing an authorized edition of *The Murder of Angela Dales*

High Tide's mission is to find, encourage, promote, and publish the work of authors. We are a small, woman-owned enterprise that is dedicated to the author over 50. When you buy an authorized copy, you help us to bring their work to you.

We thank you for supporting our authors.

Edited by Cindy L. Freeman cindy@cindylfreeman.com

Book Design by Firebellied Frog Graphic Design www.firebelliedfrog.com

Some content in this book was previously published as *The Murder of Angela Dales: A Question of Accountability* October 27, 2015

Printed in the United States of America

In Memory of Angela Dales

For Rebecca Cariens,

her daughter, our grandchild

Angela Dales

Contents

Introduction

When the mother of my oldest grandchild was murdered over twenty years ago, I never, in my wildest dreams, thought our tragedy would be the beginning of a series of national tragedies—an epidemic of gun violence. I never envisioned that Virginia would be the site of this country's worst school shooting on April 16, 2007, leaving thirty-two dead and at least seventeen wounded.

I never imagined that I would be sitting on the Governor's Commission to Investigate the Virginia Beach Mass Shooting of May 31, 2019, that left twelve dead and four wounded, or that, during my time on the panel, there would be other school shootings: one at Bridgewater College in Bridgewater, Virginia and the other at an elementary school in Uvalde, Texas.

I wrote the first edition of this book, thinking perhaps my words could help prevent other families from experiencing the anguish and pain my family had experienced.

I was wrong, sadly, terribly wrong.

Instead of working to keep guns away from people who are a threat to themselves and others, Virginia's legislators have opened the floodgates for anyone to buy any sort of firearm.

In Virginia, there is a law that a convicted spouse abuser must turn over his or her gun to a neutral third party. But the same law prevents law enforcement officers from following up to see if the spouse abuser complied with the order. That is beyond the ridiculous. It is just plain stupid.

In Ohio, the legislature has passed a concealed carry law requiring no background check, no training, or permit to carry a gun. So, in the Buckeye state, a person can beat up a spouse, or maybe even use a weapon to threaten or kill that spouse, and then go right out and buy another firearm. This is madness!

The victims' families want the truth, hoping to find justice through the facts. Unfortunately, they get lies; they get no truth and no justice. People in positions of trust and authority know no bounds to the extent they will lie to protect their careers and institutions.

To paraphrase John Steinbeck: the sharp pain of truth—being told your loved one has been murdered—can pass away; but the slow, eating agony of a lie never dies.

Who was Angela Denise Dales?

Angela Denise Dales was born on a cold, drizzling January day in 1969; she was buried thirty-three years later on a cold, drizzling January day. The time in between those two dates was anything but cold and drizzly. They represented the life of a remarkable young woman, a woman who contributed every day of her life to the world in which she lived. She would have contributed much more had she lived.

First Grandchild

She was the first grandchild on her mother's side of the family, and every day the doting grandparents would come to see her, bathe her, hold her, and love her. She developed a very close relationship with both of them. She nicknamed her maternal grandmother "ma-maw." As Angie grew, the older woman began to pass on the time-tested talents of the mountain people. She began to teach her beautiful young granddaughter to quilt. The two would take scraps of material and work for hours creating beautiful articles of American folk art.

Angie was also close to her paternal grandfather. He, too, was delighted with his beautiful grandchild. He raised bees and would take Angie with him to collect the honey. The two would spend hours walking along the steep paths of the lush green mountainsides, where they would laugh and play, enjoying the natural beauty of Southwestern Virginia.

Independent Streak

Angie had an independent streak. As a small child, she was never allowed out of the yard unless her parents knew where she was going. One day her mother, Sue, missed her and found her at a neighbor's place. She brought Angie home and explained that she couldn't go there without her mother's permission. Sue went back into the house, and, within minutes, Angie was gone again. This scenario happened three or four times. The last time, Sue resorted to something she rarely did: she spanked her daughter. Sue was puzzled--why would Angie deliberately disobey her mother and go to a house where there were no children? Later, Sue found out the family had a baby deer. Angie was going there to pet the fawn.

Everyone remembers the first day her or his child goes to school. It was no different for Angie's mom. Indeed, Angie's independent streak was the main characteristic of her first day at kindergarten. Sue drove her to the elementary school a few miles down the road. When they pulled into the parking lot, the proud mother started to get out of the car, but Angie looked at her mom and said, "Just let me out, and I will go in by myself."

There are many beautiful things to remember about Angie, but once you met her, you would never forget the intelligence, life, and enthusiasm that shone in her eyes.

A month or two before Angela's murder, she came home from school and said, "Mom, I guess you know I am an organ donor." Her mother responded, "Whatever possessed you to do that?"

"Don't tell me no. If something ever happens to me, I won't need them anymore, and I could help someone." On January 16, 2002, her eyes were taken from her dead body to help two other people see.

Neesee

Angie's family called her "Neesee." She got the nickname from her grandfather, who, as he grew older, had trouble saying Angela or Denise—so he shortened it to "Neesee" and it stuck. The nickname carries so much love that the Dales can hardly say it without tears welling in their eyes. At times we can talk about the shooting; at other times, even her name's mention immobilizes us.

Indeed, it was three years after the shooting, three long years, before the doctors finally found a medicine to help Danny Dales deal with his depression and uncontrolled sobbing. One could not measure the depth of Danny's love for his daughter.

Angie loved flowers and plants. Sue Dales never paid much attention to them before, but since Angie's death, she looks at nature and sees "Neesee." She sees why Angie loved flowers and plants so much. Sue now takes time to enjoy the magnificent beauty of southwestern Virginia's flora. She finds comfort in this beauty as if her daughter were in some small way back with her.

There is a saying that once a person who loves plants dies, no one can take the plants and keep them alive. Angie's favorite houseplant was the Christmas cactus. After her death, her mother took several plants and gave us the rest. One by one, the leaves on all the Christmas cacti dried up and turned brown. Despite all efforts, the plants were dead within a year of January 16, 2002.

Angie was Sue's first child and only daughter. Sue bore her and raised her. Yet there were aspects she could only guess about Angie. Facts and details have emerged since her death. It seems Sue never understood the true magnificence of the child she had brought into this world.

Angie's Friends

Rebecca went to live with Sue and Danny after the shooting. During the day, when the seven-year-old was in school, Sue felt like she would lose her mind. The walls closed in on her. Sue needed something to keep her busy, to maintain her sanity. Work was the answer. So Sue returned to her restaurant. One day a young man who had gone to school with Angie came into Sue's restaurant for lunch. He and his wife sat at a table near the window. Sue recognized him as one of Angie's friends from school and walked over. They began to chat.

The short conversation that ensued spoke volumes about Angie's character. The young man told Sue that when he was in high school, Angie and one of her friends had bought him a coat. It was winter, his family was poor, and he had no coat to combat the bitter mountain cold. Angie and the young man never dated, they just knew each other, and Angie knew he needed the coat. Sue had never heard the story and, to this day, has no idea where Angie got the money.

In recounting the story about the man in the restaurant, Sue told me that even three years after the shooting, she missed Angie so much that the pain was sometimes overwhelming. The stories are both comforting and unbearable. The pain of Angie's loss is there every day of the week; it will not go away. Sue is trying to learn to live with it. Every morning Sue and Danny would get up early, have coffee, sit for an hour, and try to comfort and console each other and remember Angie.

Angie Growing Up

Sue and Danny remember their beautiful daughter growing up. They recall that she rarely played with dolls; she liked music, books, and writing stories. In music, John Lennon was her hero. Their child was a beautiful blonde drum majorette who graduated third in her class and earned a full Presidential Scholarship to college.

They remember the night Angie followed the family dog into the dark pine forest on the mountainside above their house. They recall their panic when they realized she was lost and it was getting dark. They remember the sound of her crying that led them to her just as it was getting dark—they long for those cries so they can find her and bring her back once more. They wake up hearing those cries and think Angie is calling them.

Joe and Angie

Angie and her younger brother, Joe, developed a close relationship, but they would argue the way siblings do. We all long to hear those arguments once more.

Joe was born three years after Angie. Despite the arguing, when push came to shove, they were always there for each other. Sue cannot help but smile when she remembers Angie bringing back eggs from North Carolina and convincing Joe that they would hatch if he sat on them all day. The young boy did as his sister said—much to Angie's delight.

Angie was in the band in high school, and Joe was on the football team. Since she was a drum major, the siblings were together even in their after-school activities.

Joe was very protective of his older sister, closely scrutinizing any boy she brought home. If he did not care for the young man or felt he was not good enough for his sister, Joe would not hesitate to tell him so. Then when Joe started dating, it was Angie's turn. Angie would drive Joe and his girlfriend to the movies—this time, it was her turn to scrutinize and judge.

Every Christmas, the two would pick out the family tree. The process seemed to take forever; Angie liked tall trees, and Joe liked the short ones. The debate over choosing the "right tree" was involved, never rushed, and sometimes heated. One year, unable to reach an agreement, they came home with two trees.

There was never a birthday or holiday that the two were not together. The siblings already had their plans made for the future. When Angie finished law school, she would go to Bluefield, set up a practice near Joe, and handle all his legal work.

Danny laughed with tears running down his face whenever he remembered the time he had his Camaro painted bright red. Angie was just learning to drive, and he let her drive it. She ended up taking a joy ride through the lawn, shrubs, and bushes with the family running behind her, yelling for her to stop. The new paint was a mess. But when Danny looked back on the incident, he could not help but think that you can always get a new car, but you can never replace a child.

Elizabeth, the Cat

Sue can still see Angie with her cat, Elizabeth. Angie's cousin lived next door and had a tiny gray kitten. Angie would entice the cat over every day until finally, her cousin put a red ribbon around its neck and gave it to Angie. The problem was that Angie was allergic to cats and dogs, but that didn't stop her from having pets. They kept the cat in a small room off the kitchen. Despite her parent's warnings and protests, Angie couldn't resist. She would slip into the small room when no one was looking, pet the cat, and then emerge with swollen eyes and itching skin.

Angie moved into her own house when she could and took her cat along. The house was near the railroad tracks, and Angie was so afraid a train would hit her cat Elizabeth that she took the cat back to her parents for safekeeping. But it wasn't only Elizabeth's safety that bothered Angie. The long coal trains that wound through the deep gorge where she lived were a particular problem. The trains would block the road she lived on and make her late for work or class. Under the law, trains can remain stationary for no longer than thirty minutes blocking a crossing. That was not good enough for Angie. More than once, wearing high heels, she would run down the gravel track bed, climb into the engine's cab, and insist the train move. She was late for class! The train always moved.

As a youngster growing up in the mountains of southwestern Virginia, Angie had a friend with a bad home life. The young friend spent a great deal of time with Angie. The friend later recounted that it was Angie who had helped her get through the rough spots. Angie inspired her to go to college and get an education.

Angie's Poetry

At Virginia Intermont College, Angie was an honor student and received nearly every award the school had to offer. She carried a double major: English/Creative Writing and History/Political Science. Angie was one of the first five students to participate in the school's Worrell Honors Program for Studies Abroad, traveling to Munich. She spent three weeks in Germany attending lectures and studying the early development of the Nazi Party.

Angie was assistant editor of the school literary magazine, The Moore Street Review. She regularly contributed poems to the publication. In her poetry, you can see the caring, sensitive nature of an exceptionally talented young woman. She was at Virginia Intermont at the time of Desert Storm and wrote the following poem about a young man going off to war:

82nd Airborne

The engine hummed,
like steady breathing of a sleeping baby.
Dad threw the last wrench
Into a scarred toolbox.

"There ye go, son. She's ready."
Never once
looking at my blue uniform
hanging
In the window of my red Chevy.

Mom steps around the corner of the garage.
A little brown bag lunch for the road,
like Sundays going back to school.
Water laced with salt
trickles from her bloodshot eyes.
One last hug—
disappears around the corner.

Dad grips my hand
tight—breaking my bones.
"Good luck, son. Take care. Don't give'm
too much of a rough time."

Trying to laugh.
Squeezes my shoulder
with vice-like grip—
disappears around the corner.

Both now
stand in the bay window
watching
my red truck
disappear.

In another poem, Angie's love for her mother inspired her to write about the fall of the year, her favorite time. In her poem, she thanks her mother by comparing their hands. Angie thanks her mother's hands for all their hard work that gave Angie her sweet life and helped to make her the person that she became.

Contrasts

November
red and yellow leaves
fall
from sleeping trees.
Mom bakes pies
from cherries picked in June,
humming a hymn:

"Softly and Tenderly."
Her pink flowered apron—stained:
short thick hands,

coarse and calloused;
fingernails
broken and uneven.

Me—
hands
smooth and clean,
smelling of sweet lotion;
fingernails
long, painted,
as if they grew that shade of pink.

Law School Recruiter

Before becoming a student at the Appalachian School of Law, Angie joined the school's administrative staff as a recruiter. She threw herself into the work with all the enthusiasm she could muster. She worked overtime, evenings, and weekends without pay.

Her mother chastised her, saying, "The school doesn't care, the school won't be grateful. You will get no money. They won't appreciate it." Angie responded, "I'm not doing it for the school. I'm doing it for the students."

After the funeral, several students approached the Dales to say how much they appreciated Angie, how much they liked her, and how much she had done for them. When they arrived on campus for the first time, Angie was the one who was there to help—"a welcoming face, a helpful hand."

"She made us feel welcome," one student remembered, choking back tears.

The first year Angie was in law school, she joined a study group of single parents. One young woman later recounted that when her son was in the hospital, she could not attend the group and missed many of her classes. It was Angie who brought her assignments to the hospital room. Often, it was Angie who stayed with the sick child when his mother could not be there.

While Angie's brother was opening his chiropractic office right after getting out of school, his computer failed. He mentioned it in passing, and within hours Angie had driven the hour-and-a-half from Grundy to Bluefield with her computer. All she said was, "Here, Joe, keep it as long as you need it."

In relating these stories to me, stories of how Angie was always there to help someone in need, Danny told me that he gave each of his children a piece of sculpture when they were young. To Joe, he gave a coal miner statue because he wanted his son to remember his roots. He gave "Praying Hands" to Angie because he wanted his daughter always to be there to extend a helping hand to anyone who needed it.

Danny Dales was immensely proud of his children. He worked in the coal mines, crouching and crawling through the deep mine shafts literally to scratch out a living and give his children a better life. Sue recounts how Danny—after working in the grime and grit, in the foul air that would eventually give him black lung—would get dressed up on Saturday and take his beautiful little girl into town. He wanted to show off his treasure, his pride. With Angie's hand in his, he said he was the richest man in the world.

Danny's philosophy was to ensure his children had the education to give them a better chance at life, an advantage he never had. His philosophy was simple, genuine, and embodied the American dream. Danny Dales succeeded where many have failed.

The Good Die Young

There is an old adage that the good die young—certainly, that is true in Angie's case. The examples of her kindness are everywhere. In the months before the shootings, when students were raising money to help Peter Odighizuwa buy food for his family, Angie donated what she could. Ironically, she shared what little she had to help feed the family of the man who later murdered her.

When you drive up to the Dales' house, you are met by a little blonde mutt named Cinderella. A few years before her murder, Angie was on her way to night school at Radford University—three hours from Grundy. Near Bluefield, Virginia, a woman was giving away three puppies. Angie stopped, took a liking to one dog, and thought it would be a perfect gift for her daughter, Rebecca.

She took the pup, turned around, drove the hour back to Grundy, put a red ribbon around the dog's neck, and gave it to Rebecca. She then returned to Radford.

Angie and my wife shared this love for animals. During Angie's last visit, we had a small dog named Mike in our foster care. Neither man nor nature had been kind to Mike. He was aggressive and hard to like. He really didn't look like a dog. He was short and round, with a pushed-in face. One ear stood up, and the other flopped over. He looked more like a pig than a dog. Indeed, that is what one of the neighbors nicknamed him, "the pig."

We found Mike wandering near our home. His previous owner had cut off his tail, exposing a piece of bone. My wife had the tail operated on and nursed Mike back to health. We found homes for him three times, and the new owners brought him back three times. He tore up lawns, chewed on furniture, and was not particularly affectionate; in short, he had nothing to recommend him. Some even volunteered that the dog was psychotic. He was hard to love, hard to be around. Not for Angie. She was incredibly loving and caring toward Mike, and the dog responded in kind.

When Angie left our house after our last Christmas together, Mike broke loose and chased her car. Unable to lure Mike back, Janice and I waved goodbye and watched Angie's car disappear with the little "pig" following her. Not far down the road, Angie got Mike into her car and brought him back. All we know is that when we came outside later that day, Mike was safe inside our lawn with the gate closed.

Memories of Angie are all around us—everywhere we look. These memories live on; they will never leave. We remember how excited she was about the prospect of a law school opening in Grundy. She was probably the biggest promoter of Grundy and the law school outside the Chamber of Commerce. To this day, I can hear the excitement in her beautiful, gentle southern accent as she talked about the school, her home, and the mountains of southwestern Virginia. How wonderful the school would be! From the word of its founding, she was determined to enroll, to get her law degree.

As soon as the school opened, Angie applied for and got a job in the Appalachian School of Law's recruiting office. She traveled throughout the Southeastern United States and played a critical role in attracting students to the fledgling institution. Who could have possibly known that the school she loved so much, the school she was so proud of, would eventually be the site of her death?

On January 16, 2002, Angela Denise Dales' last day alive, she took her daughter Rebecca to her parents' house to wait for the school bus. She always made sure that Rebecca's day had a good start. Angela's mother watched out the window as the two laughed and played. Once Rebecca was safely on the school bus, Angie went back inside the house, as she always did, said goodbye, and headed home to prepare for the day's classes. That afternoon, three bullets fired by Peter Odighizuwa ended her life.

"Never too old to Learn from Children."

Danny Dales later said, "You are never too old to learn; to learn from children." We raise our children and teach them; then they grow up and teach us. Danny said he always thought he knew what love was, "but Angie taught me what love really was. She taught me to love flowers, nature, rain, and snow. She taught me to love and appreciate all the things we take for granted."

Once someone's life is tragically taken, particularly a young person's life, we spend hours and days remembering. All of us, the Dales and Cariens, spend time remembering Angela. At times the pain and anguish are so horrific that you think you will lose your mind. You experience a catharsis. There is no place you can go to escape the memories. A memory that once was so happy is now bitter.

Everything in life is turned on its head. The tragedy acts as a filter. It filters your priorities and your values; it filters your friends—you learn whom you can count on. Just when you think you can move ahead, a smell or a word reminds you of the lost one. The horror of what happened comes flooding back with all the force and impact of when you first learned about the tragedy. Just when you think you can move on, a black cloud envelops you, and all the pain rushes in. You can be driving along on a bright, beautiful spring day. All's right with the world. Then it hits you. Nothing is right; everything is wrong. The loss you have suffered means that nothing will ever be right again.

I'm not sure why tragedies of this proportion have such an impact on the brain, but suddenly your senses seem so acute that you remember the tragedy in every detail—you relive everything. You recall the instant you heard the news—every smell, every color, the temperature—everything.

The Murderer

It was January 16, 2002, when a toxic mix of hatred, mental illness, incompetence, and arrogance came together with deadly consequences.

Who is Peter Odighizuwa?

He is a native of Nigeria who came to this country looking for a better life. He was and is a deeply flawed individual, and these flaws were readily apparent. He had come to the U.S. at the age of twenty-two and, according to newspaper accounts, settled in Portland, Oregon, where soon he was receiving treatment for some sort of emotional or mental disorder. The reports of his early life in this country are sketchy, but a picture emerges of a man struggling to exist in the world around him. Peter Odighizuwa lacked, and lacks to this day, compassion or feelings for his fellow human beings. He is devoid of the most basic interpersonal skills.

Peter Odighizuwa may be deeply flawed, but he is not stupid. Indeed, Odighizuwa later moved to Ohio, where he received a college education. Again, the accounts of his time there are sketchy, but we know that he was prescribed the antidepressant Prozac.

By the time Peter Odighizuwa arrived in Grundy, his pattern of irrational behavior was a distinct part of his personality. He demonstrated these unstable traits both on and off the law school campus. Fellow students and townspeople who came in contact with him describe him as self-centered and boorish to the point that his paranoia was readily apparent. Words such as irrational, paranoid, bizarre, psychotic, and violent became synonymous with his name.

Peter Odighizuwa's behavior indicated that he not only needed professional help but was wholly unsuited for interaction with other humans on a professional, much less polite, or casual level of conduct.

Violent Outbursts

Soon after Odighizuwa's arrival on campus, his violent outbursts against school staff, faculty, and fellow students became well known. It was easier for the school to rationalize his aberrant behavior than attract other minority students. The Appalachian School of Law needed minority students to gain accreditation from the American Bar Association, so it appears that it was willing to bend over backward to be tolerant. Admitting Odighizuwa, a black, naturalized U.S. citizen, would help the school reach its required quota.

Multiple reports of erratic behavior exhibited by Odighizuwa during his one-and-a-half years at the school—both on and off the campus—constitute strong evidence that nearly everyone in Grundy knew of his unstable behavior. For example, during his first semester at school in the fall of 2000, he pushed Professor Paul Lund from his classroom lectern and took control of the class for approximately ten minutes. Later, Odighizuwa reportedly verbally attacked and threatened a female student, Michelle Ray, during Professor C. Wesley Shinn's class.

Assault Charges

On August 15, 2000, Odighizuwa was charged with assault against his wife and appeared before the Buchanan County Juvenile & Domestic Relations District Court. There were unconfirmed reports that school officials unofficially offered him legal advice. Later, in October 2001, just three months before the deadly shooting rampage, Odighizuwa's wife was granted a protective order against her husband by a local magistrate of the Juvenile & Domestic Relations District Court.

Shirley Trent Stanley lived next door to the Odighizuwas. The press quoted her as saying that Mrs. Odighizuwa and the four children had many friends. However, Odighizuwa was a "peculiar neighbor who frequently complained that he was harassed wherever he went." She added, "He stayed in the house… you didn't see him outside."

Throughout the fall of 2000, community members, including the principal where Odighizuwa's children attended school, reportedly expressed fear of him.

That same fall, he verbally abused an employee of the law school library, Anita Stanley. Ms. Stanley filed a formal complaint, a grievance with the school expressing fear for her safety. Reportedly, her complaint explicitly stated that she feared bodily harm. Odighizuwa confronted her as she vacuumed the library and ordered her to stop. Had it not been for the intervention of another student, Ms. Stanley believed Odighizuwa would have hurt her.

There is also an account that Odighizuwa threatened Vicki Keene, a school employee, who passed the incident report to school authorities. Ms. Keene, too, feared for her safety. Indeed, she was so afraid that, in this instance, the school took action and banned Odighizuwa from her office. Odighizuwa also reportedly "screamed at" Associate Professor Wendy Davis during one of her classes. Professor Davis filed a complaint with the law school president,

Dr. Lucius Ellsworth. But, she is quoted by Ron Coleman in his book, *The Appalachian School of Law Murders*, as declining to discuss Peter Odighizuwa's behavior, claiming she did not make formal complaints to anyone at the school.

During his second semester on campus, Odighizuwa's outbursts continued unabated. He verbally attacked students, staff, and faculty. Press reports indicate that during that time, he cursed at a staff member, calling her "a goddamn bitch" and saying "fuck you," then adding that he hoped the place "would go to the dogs." When informed of this incident, School President Ellsworth reportedly said, "It's okay. Just ignore him."

Conflicts Escalate

The killer's campus tirades continued throughout the fall of 2001. During that period, he visited the Student Services office to ask for money, and, when his requests were not met, he cursed out Chris Clifton, the financial-aid director. Clifton repeatedly told Odighizuwa that there was nothing he could do. He could award Odighizuwa no more financial aid. According to Clifton, Dean Sutin had helped Odighizuwa get a $19,000.00 loan in the fall before the shooting. Odighizuwa would now have to pay back that loan and others.

Clifton recounts that the distraught student responded with screams, calling staff members names. Clifton did not file a formal complaint but informed Dean Sutin of the incident. Clifton would later recount to the press that Odighizuwa came into his office and was verbally abusive on Tuesday, the day before the shooting. "He was very hostile," Clifton said. The press also quoted Clifton saying, "This student had previously threatened the entire Office of Student Services. He had even stolen his file once before." Clifton added, "I think Peter knew it [his dismissal] was going to be permanent and final. He slung his chair across the room and slammed the door."

In October 2001, Odighizuwa threatened another law student, Matthew Tham, who reported this incident to school authorities.

As a result of Odighizuwa's verbal explosion, he was barred from entering the Office of Student Services unless the president of the Student Bar Association or the dean escorted him. Odighizuwa ignored the order and continued to enter the office and harass its employees.

Odighizuwa's violent outbursts prompted some students to give him the nickname "the shooter" because they feared he would "go postal." Others reportedly refused to sit in front of him in class because they feared he would bring a gun to school someday and start shooting.

Shortly after the shooting spree, one student, Kenneth Brown, told the press his friends had joked that Odighizuwa was one of those guys who would finally crack and bring a gun to school. "He was kind of off-balance," Brown reportedly said. "When we met last year, he actually came up and shook my hand and asked my name. Then, like five minutes later, he came back and said, 'You know I'm not crazy, but people tick me off sometimes.' Out of the blue."

Odighizuwa's paranoid tendencies were apparent to anyone who met him. Another student, Zeke Jackson, said, "I stopped trying to recruit Odighizuwa for the school's Black Law Students' Association after he sent the dean a letter complaining that I was harassing him."

The press quoted Jackson as saying, "I thought he was going to hurt a student. I thought he was going to lash out at a student. He had been explosive when he was told he was wrong. I feel kind of guilty. I really wish I had gone to the dean of students or somebody and said, 'You need to get rid of this guy.'" Jackson also described Odighizuwa as having an "abrasive, everyone-is-against-me attitude."

Female Staff Members File Complaints

According to court documents filed in Wise County, Virginia, three female staff members filed a complaint with school officials against Odighizuwa, expressing fear for their safety and the safety of others at the school. These court documents also assert that the women aired their complaint at a school administrative meeting. The school's top three officials—President Lucius Ellsworth, Dean L. Anthony Sutin, and Associate Dean Paul Lund—were said to attend the meeting. The same documents assert that Ellsworth responded to the complaint by saying, "You women and your hormones and your intuition… there is nothing for you to be afraid of…it will be okay."

Dr. Briggs, the same physician who was one of the first to arrive at the school after the shooting, later acknowledged that he had treated Odighizuwa. The press quoted Briggs as saying, "I had no idea that it [stress] would affect him this way…. He was a time bomb waiting to go off." Dr. Briggs is also quoted as describing the association between Odighizuwa and Dean Sutin as "a parasitic relationship." He meant that Dean Sutin had bent over backward to help Odighizuwa. There are reports that he even bought him a computer and ensured Odighizuwa had enough financial assistance to cover his tuition. Dr. Briggs is also quoted as saying that Odighizuwa "came here poverty-stricken and slept on the floor. People helped them [Peter, his wife, and four children]. There would be no academic institution that would allow him to come in on that basis that I know of." It would appear that all of Grundy, including the Appalachian School of Law, knew about Peter Odighizuwa's aberrant behavior.

Mental Instability Well Known

Indeed, Odighizuwa's penchant for violence was known even in Richmond. The morning after the shooting, Virginia Governor Mark Warner's spokesperson admitted to the news media that Odighizuwa "had a history of mental instability that school officials knew about." The governor was a member of the Board of Trustees of the Law School at the time of the shooting.

Odighizuwa's irrational behavior was apparent in all aspects of his life. For example, he reported several false claims to the police. One of his reports filed during this time claimed that someone had put a bullet in a stairway in his home. Sheriff's Chief Deputy Randall Ashby told the press that Odighizuwa had also reported to police in the year before the shooting that someone had broken into his home.

The police checked out these complaints and found nothing. Odighizuwa regularly visited the sheriff's office to nitpick with deputies over the police reports he filed.

Odighizuwa had a problem with women, particularly intelligent women and women in authority. This may have been part of his African heritage. In some cultures, women are still treated as the property of men. They are bought, sold, sexually abused, disfigured, and even murdered. In some circles, it may not be politically correct to acknowledge these facts, but they are true.

The stage was set for a tragedy.

All the signs were there.

Two days before the shooting, on January 14, 2002, Odighizuwa had gone to school to pick up his grades. He had failed. The previous year, he had been allowed to withdraw voluntarily and then re-enroll. This year, there would be no withdrawal option. The school put his grades in his mailbox to prevent a scene. But, the disgruntled student went to the Student Services Office. Staff members recall him being highly agitated. He began cursing and stormed out. The commotion was so loud that other staff members came out of their offices to see what was happening. Odighizuwa stormed out in what can only be described as a hysterical rage. Checking on the altercation, Dean Sutin reportedly asked if anyone knew where he was. The press reports that one of the staff members responded, "Well, he's probably over at the bell tower in the courthouse with a scope."

The news that he had failed school meant that Odighizuwa lost all financial aid. He was desperate. Chris Clifton, the school's financial officer, met with Odighizuwa on Tuesday, January 15th to permanently dismiss him for poor grades. His dismissal meant that Odighizuwa, who had been allowed to withdraw the year before (and then be readmitted), would have to repay $9,250 in federal school loans. Odighizuwa was broke, desperate, and unbalanced. The news must have been overwhelming, suffocating. I have not read any accounts of what he did in the days immediately preceding the shootings. I doubt that any exist. Given his unstable nature, I would guess that panic triggered his subsequent actions.

After Odighizuwa met with Clifton, he drove some forty miles to Southwest Virginia Community College seeking work. He had tried several times to find a job at the college teaching math. While his credentials were impressive, the school did not need an instructor, and he was—again—turned down. His panic and desperation must have reached incredible proportions.

The Shooting

On January 16th, Peter Odighizuwa was at the law school early. He should not have been there—he had no business on the school grounds. In effect, he was trespassing; he had flunked out. At about 8 o'clock, a student saw Odighizuwa in the school parking lot and told Dean Sutin that Peter was on the grounds. Sutin reportedly brushed the news aside. The dean was busy preparing for his 9 o'clock lecture.

Students Reported Shooter was Agitated

Other students reported seeing him on campus various times during that fateful morning. Later, one student said he saw Odighizuwa in the library calmly reading a newspaper; another reported seeing him walking back and forth nervously outside Professor Blackwell's classroom. Odighizuwa's agitated pacing caught Blackwell's eye. The professor stopped the class, went to the door, and reportedly said something to him. Odighizuwa disappeared down the hall.

September 16th

Around 11:00 am on the sixteenth, Peter Odighizuwa went to Professor Dale Rubin's office, where the two men got into a heated argument. The verbal confrontation lasted some thirty minutes. Documents filed at the Wise County courthouse indicate that Professor Rubin knew about Odighizuwa's failing grades, that he was "emotionally distraught," and that Odighizuwa had exhibited past and present mental problems and emotional outbursts.

The same court documents assert that "Rubin, who had a reputation for being antagonistic, riling up and provoking people, and would regularly use profanity and obscene language in his classroom and make degrading remarks towards students, admitted that he knew at the time that Odighizuwa was very upset with Dean Anthony Sutin." Professor Rubin later acknowledged to the press that he knew Odighizuwa was upset and might hit Dean Sutin.

After the shooting, Professor Rubin was quoted as saying that he thought Odighizuwa might "…go cuss Sutin out or throw a punch at him…." but "didn't think that he would kill him." The court document states, "Notwithstanding Odighizuwa's mental status of rage and Rubin's knowledge of Odighizuwa's physical and verbal outrages, Rubin failed to contact law enforcement officers or school personnel regarding the alarming condition of Odighizuwa, and he failed to take any precautions for the safety of the law school students, faculty, staff, and others. The court document continues, "Instead, he [Rubin] casually left the law school and went to lunch without even attempting to warn Dean Sutin or making any attempt to determine if Odighizuwa was still on the law school premises, and without warning anyone of Odighizuwa's rage and his request to 'pray for me.'"

After the shooting, in court filings, Professor Rubin claimed that he had no duty to warn anyone that Odighizuwa was angry. Furthermore, Rubin asserted that Odighizuwa's acts were not foreseeable by him.

Nevertheless, the sad truth is that Odighizuwa's meeting with Professor Rubin may have been the last chance to prevent the tragedy. Within hours Odighizuwa shot to death Rubin's two former rivals for the position of Dean of Students.

After the confrontation between Professor Rubin and Odighizuwa, the disgruntled, unstable student returned home and got his gun.

Killing Dean Anthony Sutin

At around 1:00 in the afternoon, Peter Odighizuwa returned to the law school campus, bent on revenge against all he perceived were denying him his education in law.

At 1:15 pm, Professor Gail Kintzer sat in her second-floor office two doors away from Professor Blackwell's office. She heard two pops and immediately knew they were gunshots. Her office door opened, and two hysterical secretaries ran in: Melanie Lewis, Dean Sutin's secretary, and Donna Horn, a faculty secretary. The two women had just witnessed Odighizuwa's execution-style shooting of Dean Sutin. The gunman had shot Sutin twice. The powder burn indicated he was shot at close range from behind. He was shot a third time in the side. The bloodstains on the dean's white shirt told the terrible truth—he was dead.

Dean Sutin was a graduate of Brandeis University and Harvard University School of Law. He had served as a deputy associate U.S. attorney general during the Clinton administration and worked for the Democratic National Committee and the 1992 Clinton presidential campaign.

Anthony Sutin was an over-achiever. That is the way friends remember him growing up. He was bright and made excellent grades in high school. From his early, formative years, he was devoted to doing things to make the world better. For example, he worked for several environmental causes.

Sutin had brought his family to this small, blue-collar, economically depressed Southwest Virginia community believing that he could make a difference in people's lives. He taught constitutional law I and II. The school had been established to give hope and opportunity to the people of this region. It was a calling that Dean Sutin and his family shared and were accomplishing. He left behind his wife, Margaret Lawton, and two small children, Henry and Clara. Clara, at the time, was a fourteen-month-old from China that Professor Sutin and his wife had adopted just one month before the shooting.

"He's Got a Gun!"

"He's got a gun!" Lewis and Kintzer screamed and crawled under the professor's desk. When Professor Kintzer tried to phone for help, all the emergency numbers were busy.

The Roanoke Times and *World News* quoted Professor Wes Shinn, whose office was next to Blackwell's, saying that he too heard the noise, opened his door, and saw the two horrified secretaries standing in the hall. They were screaming, "He's got a gun; he's got a gun!"

Shinn slammed his door and was later quoted as saying that he assumed Odighizuwa was going office-to-office executing the faculty one after another. He then heard two more shots farther down the hall. Apparently feeling the danger was moving away from him, Shinn said he opened the door slowly and peered into the hallway. Deciding it was relatively safe, he went to Professor Blackwell's office.

Killing Professor Thomas Blackwell

Professor Thomas Blackwell was, by all accounts, the most popular faculty member on campus. He taught contracts, intellectual property, law office management practicum, and legal process. Of all the staff and faculty, Professor Blackwell was the man Angela Dales admired the most; she often commented how much she admired him and loved his classes. He was only forty-one years old—two years younger than the man who murdered him. A graduate of the University of Texas at Arlington and Duke University School of Law, Professor Blackwell and his family became part of the Grundy community. He and his wife, Lisa, sang in their church choir. His children regularly helped out at the Mountain Mission School for orphans and children in extreme poverty. Professor Blackwell is survived by his wife and three children, daughter Jillian, and sons Zeb and Zeke.

As Professor Blackwell talked on the phone to Charlotte Varney, his church secretary, Odighizuwa burst into his office, continuing his murderous rampage. Blackwell was active in the Buchanan First Presbyterian Church, and the two were discussing an upcoming congregational meeting. When Blackwell stopped talking, Varney reported hearing something like a paper bag popping; she heard the phone drop and static. "I asked him what was going on, but he didn't come back on the line," she said.

After a couple of minutes, she hung up the phone and ran an errand. It was half an hour before she learned what had happened.

Blackwell was sitting slumped over his desk, bleeding from the neck. Shinn approached his motionless body and checked for a pulse. He found none. Despite all his and Dean Sutin's good work and efforts to bring hope to this struggling, poverty-ridden community, both men now lay dead in pools of blood on a bone-chilling Wednesday afternoon in 2002.

No one on the first floor was aware of what had happened over their heads or what form of hell was about to descend on them. Some students were still eating lunch in the Lion's Lounge, the first-floor student lounge. Others were returning to campus to prepare for the afternoon schedule of classes. Some fifteen to twenty students sat on sofas and chairs, chatting and laughing. A few others walked through on their way to classes.

The press reported that Arun Rattan, a first-year student, had just returned from lunch at the Italian Village, a downtown restaurant frequented by students and staff. He was with Stacey Bean and her boyfriend, James Davis. Bean, a pretty, intelligent blonde, would become one of Odighizuwa's targets.

Rattan remembers sensing movement behind him and turned to see Odighizuwa standing next to him. He remembers thinking that it appeared Odighizuwa had just come down the steps from Dean Sutin's office. He had, and on the way, he had casually talked to students in the stairwell as if nothing had happened.

Odighizuwa nodded at Rattan and walked past him. Rattan noticed he had a gun but later recalled that it did not register what was going on or what was about to happen.

Killing Angela Dales

Angie Dales had canceled a lunch date to do some reading in preparation for her afternoon classes. Angie was everything Odighizuwa hated in women—she was bright, popular, made good grades, and had held a responsible position at the law school. He targeted her.

Entering the student lounge, he chatted briefly with a Black student body member. Then Odighizuwa spotted Angie, Rebecca Brown, and Madeline Short sitting on a sofa across the room. He walked diagonally around several students within a few feet of Angie Dales. He fired three bullets into her at point-blank range. Later he would say that she had not been nice to him—a feeble, demented justification for taking a human life. Standing about five feet from the three women, he fired at Angela Dales first. Witnesses said she raised her arm to protect herself, but she could not stop the bullets from piercing her neck, chest, and shoulder.

At his sentencing, the press reported Peter Odighizuwa's "rage had since boiled away, and now he wept with the teenage son of one of the slain victims. Choking on tears, he said he was sorry." The press did not tell the public that shortly before his sentencing, in talks with the victim's attorney, this same Peter Odighizuwa gloated that all three victims "got what they deserved."

Bleeding profusely, Angie staggered across the hall, pleading for help. The room erupted in screams, and pandemonium ensued. As she crossed the room, Angela Dales repeatedly called out, "Please don't let me die; I have a little girl!"

While bullets had hit none of her vital organs, she was seriously wounded. The hospital was less than three minutes away, and if she could get there, she might be saved.

In a valiant effort to help her reach safety, Angie's fellow students pulled her into the doorway of the Career Services Office. One, a former nurse, tried to treat her wounds and stop the bleeding, but Angie needed blood; she required emergency room treatment. As others evacuated, Angela Dales lay dying on the floor. She bled to death when her lungs filled with blood. It was too late by the time she was evacuated—nearly forty minutes after the shooting. Angela Dales died within minutes of reaching the hospital. Her death certificate states that she was shot at 1:16 pm and died at 2:06 pm.

Madeline Short

Bullets slammed into Madeline Short's body, entering her back and ripping through her abdomen and liver. She slumped to the floor. Rebecca Brown, seriously wounded in the abdomen, managed to crawl through a window and ran to the library.

Stacy Bean

Peter Odighizuwa turned his twisted, demented rage on Stacy Bean and shot her in the chest. He targeted only women.

The once calm, pleasant student lounge turned into a blood-spattered war zone. The room looked like a slaughterhouse, the site of mass killings. Police investigators were later quoted as saying they had never seen anything like it.

Outside, a spectacle of panic and pandemonium greeted students returning to campus. Their colleagues were climbing through first-floor windows and running out the door shouting, "He's got a gun, he's got a gun!"

Mikael Gross was walking back from lunch with friends when they heard the gunshots. They saw and listened to the chaos. Gross remembers hearing something whiz by him. It was a bullet that went through Dean Sutin's window.

Gross ran to his car and retrieved a bulletproof vest and a 9 mm handgun. He had been a police officer in the Grafton, North Carolina Police Department. By the time he returned, Odighizuwa had put down his gun and ammunition clip.

Student Ted Besen had been inside the building on the second floor waiting for classes to start when he heard the shots. Besen, a former marine and Wilmington, N.C. police officer, along with fellow student Tracey Bridges, another former police officer, were on the second-floor waiting for their classes to start. The two men ran into the hallway, where they saw a professor shouting, "Peter is in the building shooting."

Ted Besen and Tracey Bridges

Hearing muffled gunshots, Bridges and Besen helped students down the stairs to safety. Then they went around the building, staying close to the wall, and tackled Odighizuwa. There are conflicting reports about what happened next. Bridges had run to his truck to retrieve a handgun. Some reports say Bridges returned, gun in hand, confronted Odighizuwa and told him to put down his weapon. Other witnesses say that Besen confronted Odighizuwa, and a fight ensued. No matter the exact sequence, it is clear a scuffle ensued. At one point, Todd Ross, another student, ran up and tackled Odighizuwa by the legs causing all three men, Besen, Odighizuwa, and Ross, to fall to the ground. More students joined the fray. Another student sat on Odighizuwa as former police officer Gross returned to his car to get handcuffs.

Gun-rights activists seized on the question of when Bridges retrieved his gun and its role in subduing Odighizuwa. Eyewitnesses said Odighizuwa was already on the ground when Bridges showed up. Frankly, when the gun appeared does not make much difference. What matters is that Odighizuwa was prevented from continuing his killing rampage. What also makes a difference is that shrill right-wing gun activists seized this point and quashed a discussion on how Virginia laws allowed a mentally disturbed wife abuser to own a gun in the first place.

Most of Odighizuwa's mutterings were unintelligible, but students reported hearing him say, "I had to do it. I didn't know what else to do. I had nowhere else to go."

Melissa McCall-Burton, a former emergency room nurse, returned to the campus from lunch around 1:30 pm. Grabbing her medical bag from her car, she ran to the student lounge. The first victim she saw was Angela Dales lying near the Career Services Office doorway.

Dr. Jack Briggs

McCall-Burton started working on her, but Angie went into cardiac arrest. McCall-Burton was performing cardiopulmonary resuscitation when Dr. Jack Briggs, nurse practitioner Susan Looney, and registered nurse Carol Breeding arrived. Dr. Briggs took one look and said he could do nothing. He is quoted as saying that a bullet severed the carotid artery. "You could put pressure on it, but you couldn't stop the bleeding. She was hemorrhaging. She was expected to die." The autopsy report, however, clearly refutes that. The report makes no mention of a pierced carotid artery. She bled to death.

Dr. Briggs recognized that all four women were seriously wounded and needed blood. For reasons that remain a mystery, the town's ambulance dispatcher evidently told the driver not to divert from his routine call to the school. All four wounded students needed blood—Angie, the most seriously wounded victim, needed it immediately. Angela Dales might be alive today if she had been the first to be evacuated.

Eyewitness accounts indicate that school officials and staff were nowhere to be seen in the immediate aftermath of the shooting. In their absence, the students were left to their own devices and began the heroic task of organizing relief, first aid, and evacuation of the wounded. Chief Deputy Randy Ashby arrived on the scene and radioed for rescue vehicles. Standing on the school grounds, he saw an ambulance from the county's only private ambulance service pass, headed for the hospital on a routine call. The ambulance did not stop.

Student Stephanie Mutter backed her Toyota 4-Runner up to the lobby doors. Other students placed Madeline Short on a table where she had had coffee and donuts just hours earlier. They threw coffee and leftover donuts on the floor as the table became one of several improvised gurneys. One-by-one, the wounded students were removed, all but Angela Dales, the most seriously wounded. Without more qualified medical expertise, the students attending to Angie were reluctant to move her. They realized her wounds were severe and did not want to take any action that might result in paralysis or other long-term problems.

Medical personnel did not move Angie from the campus until nearly thirty minutes after the other three students. It was too late.

The Buchanan County Sheriff's office had called the Grundy Funeral Home asking for help. The funeral home sent four men and a hearse. Angela Dales, unconscious, barely clung to life as students loaded her into a hearse. "I wish we'd gotten Angela first," Stephanie Mutter is reported to have said when she heard that Angela had died. Perhaps somewhere in Mutter's mind, she recognized that the evacuation of the wounded from the law school had violated a basic rule of triage—the most seriously wounded are to be evacuated first.

The Family

At least once in everyone's life, you make the right decision or do something right—I mean *really* right! For weeks, months, and years, you say to yourself, "Thank God I did that!" For me, one of those decisions came in the late summer of 2001. I decided to put everything aside to complete a Christmas project that I had put off for years. I wanted the Christmas of 2001 to be special—little did I know how special. It would be our last holiday with Angie.

Christmas 2001

In the months before Christmas 2001, I put my wife on notice—no honey-do projects. Our granddaughter, Rebecca, and her mother, Angie, would be here for the holidays—I wanted it to be a Christmas to remember. Years before, I had saved a picture of a Christmas tree stand built as a train station with electric trains running around it. It reminded me that I had intended to make it but kept putting it off. This was the year.

I had grown up with an electric train around the Christmas tree. It was our family tradition, and I wanted to create the same tradition for my grandchildren. Rebecca, my oldest grandchild, was seven and would be eight in January. She was growing so fast, and I wanted her to have nothing but the best childhood memories of Christmas with her grandparents. Rebecca would be old enough to enjoy and play with the train. I can still feel my excitement when I was her age: the smell of the pine tree, the lights, the sound of the electric train running around the tree—the ideal Christmas memory all children should have and all adults should treasure in their memories.

I spent September and October building a train station out of plywood, painting it white, and trimming it in red and green. I then cut windows in the station and put red and green cellophane on them so that when the inside light was on, the station windows lit in traditional Christmas colors. Next, I fastened the station to a 4 x 4 sheet of plywood. Around it, I placed two tracks and miniature Christmas trees with traces of snow. It was anything but professional, but the result was just what I wanted—as long as no one looked too closely.

When Angie and Rebecca arrived, we placed the tree on top of the train station in the front hall. It just fit under the nine-foot ceiling. I had bought an inexpensive Lionel freight train, but the sound it made running around the tree was worth a million dollars. With only the Christmas tree lights on and the train encircling the tree, the hall looked like a Currier and Ives greeting card.

I showed Rebecca how to operate the train and told Angie not to worry. "If something gets broken, it is a toy train for my grandchildren to play with. I can always replace the train; I can never replace you or Rebecca."

Indeed, throughout the five days that they were with us, we would hear Rebecca come down the front hall steps, and in a few moments, there would be the sound of the train circling the tree. True Christmas music!

Our oldest son, David Cariens, is Rebecca's father. Unfortunately, Angie and David could not live together or even exist in the same confines for long without the most horrific arguments. For lack of any other way to explain the two of them, I referred to their relationship as a "Mediterranean marriage." They were all passion—all love or all anger. There seemed to be no in-between for the two of them.

David now lived in Newport News. He and Angie had never married. Indeed, for several years after Rebecca was born, they never spoke to each other. Their split had been bitter, and it seemed that whenever one was ready for reconciliation, the other was not, and vice versa. This Christmas, they would see each other at our house.

David and his friend, Michelle, came up from Newport News to see his daughter and spend a couple of nights. The situation was not going to be easy, but to our great relief, the two young women hit it off. The hostility and anger that usually characterized David and Angie's relationship were absent. Perhaps it was the Christmas season or Rebecca's presence. Whatever it was, the holiday gathering went well.

Several times during the days David and Angie were together, they seemed to rekindle their feelings for each other. More than once, their expressions toward each other indicated that the old passion was still there. It was almost as if they were courting again. At one point, I turned to Janice, my wife, and said, "They are still in love—I think they are going to get together after all."

Oh great! I thought. *Michelle is a wonderful young woman. What about her? What about her feelings?* As it turned out, my concerns were to become moot three weeks later.

During Angie's visit, we made plans for the coming year. The following summer, she hoped to do her law school internship in Richmond. Angie would live with us, and Janice would watch Rebecca. Richmond is an hour-and-a-half drive, but that didn't bother Angie. She was excited about getting hands-on experience at a law firm. Her goal was to graduate and go into family law practice.

We talked a great deal about her classes. I was especially interested in how the school viewed the Nuremberg trials. I majored in German history in college and remembered discussions about the impact of those trials on international law. I told her that, if I recall correctly, some members of the legal profession were questioning the legality of putting leaders of a defeated enemy on trial. The problem centered on some aspect of legal precedent, but I could not remember what. I was also interested in how law schools dealt with raising the statute of limitations for apprehending and trying Nazis for genocide. I have tried repeatedly to remember Angie's response, but I simply can't.

Angie Discusses Concerns about Odighizuwa

During one conversation, Angie mentioned there was a student at the Appalachian School of Law who frightened her. His name was Peter. She recounted that he seemed to have a problem with women. But, he had issues with everyone. She told me Peter's nickname was "the shooter." When I pressed Angie about her safety, she brushed it aside, saying she would be careful. I asked her if the school knew about him. "Yes," she said. "Everyone knows about him and his irrational behavior. Everyone's a little afraid of him."

Living in Virginia, where so much U.S. history has been made, I became increasingly interested in our nation's heritage. Our son, Ben, and his fiancée, Sutopa, had given me Shelby Foote's PBS production on the Civil War. Angie was a Civil War buff, and while I had majored in history, it was European history, not American. Angie's enthusiasm for American history made me realize that I needed to learn more about the war that shaped so much of our nation's past.

Angie and I watched some of the videotapes together and planned to go to Gettysburg the following summer. She knew of an inn dating back to the War Between the States that was supposed to be haunted by a Civil War soldier. "Great! If you get me the name, I'll make reservations. Rebecca would love it." We had taken Angie and Rebecca on vacation with us the previous summer. Gettysburg would be another great family adventure.

We had so much to be thankful for and look forward to. What a fantastic holiday we had!

January 2002

Christmas had come and gone. The new year brought promise.

I have a cousin who says that January is the worst month. According to her, something terrible always happens in January. I did not see it that way. January has always been a good time to reflect and prepare for the coming year; it has always been downtime. My business is slow in January, so I am home most of the time. I enjoy the cold weather and gray skies—it is a time to sit by a fire, read, think, and prepare for all the coming year offers.

That January, there was a great deal to look forward to. Angie had called on the 11th saying she had gotten her grades–"all Bs." She could hardly contain her enthusiasm. She was in the top ranks of her first-year law class. Next semester she vowed, "to make As." She was on her way, doing something she loved. I did not talk with her, but Janice said she was excited about life and her studies; she was full of confidence and determination.

January 16, 2002

On January 16, I got up determined to deal with some business-related problems. I had received several inquiries about teaching some new writing courses. The difficulty was that a computer virus had hit us. The virus disabled my email capability. I had backup discs and paper files for all my files, so it was not as bad as it first appeared. However, I needed to send some emails answering inquiries and confirming my work schedule for the coming months.

I was determined to get on the internet but couldn't. Around 1:30 pm, I decided to call our friends, Lou and Don Swats, and ask to use their computer to answer my business emails. The answer was "yes." Shortly before 2:00 pm, I got in my truck and headed for their house. When I turned out of my driveway, I noticed it was a few minutes before the top of the hour, so I turned on the radio to catch the news.

The announcer was coming on with the lead story. He said there had been a school shooting in southwestern Virginia—in Grundy at the Appalachian School of Law. "Two faculty members and one student have been killed. Several others have been wounded."

I was stunned.

The student could be Angie—no, it couldn't—there are several hundred students at the law school. What are the chances she would be the one killed? The odds were in our favor; it could not be Angie.

I turned around at the next farm and raced home. When I reached our driveway, I began blowing the horn, driving as fast as possible. Stopping beside the house, I left the motor running and ran in the back door.

"Quick, turn on the TV. There has been a shooting at the law school in Grundy."

"No Reason to Expect the Worst"

Janice and I listened as the commentator repeated what I had heard on the radio. For one awful moment, we looked at each other in silence; we were both in shock. "Look, there is no reason to expect the worst," I said, trying to comfort my wife and myself. "What are the chances of Angie being the dead student? The odds are hundreds to one," I continued, trying to reassure both of us. "Keep the TV on. I'm going to the Swats. I'll call you when I get there."

Twenty minutes later, when I arrived at our friend's home, I explained what had happened and called home. The news broadcasts were still not identifying the dead student. "I'm sure the dead student is not our Angie," I told Lou and Don.

At home, by three in the afternoon, we still had no word. The news just kept repeating the same short account of the shooting. The lack of specifics, the lack of names, kept eating away at us; neither of us could relax. Finally, around 3:30, Janice said, "I cannot stand it any longer. I'm going to call Angie's brother's office. They'll know."

Joe Dales and his wife, Kay, are chiropractors in Bluefield, Virginia, about an hour-and-a-half from Grundy. Why didn't we think of this earlier? One call and our minds would be at rest.

"I am so Sorry."

Janice identified herself to the receptionist and said we had been so worried. Was Angie okay?

The words at the other end were simple, clear, and devastating, "I'm so sorry, Mrs. Cariens. I am just so sorry."

"Oh no!" is all I heard from my wife's lips. "Oh no!"

A black cloud engulfed me. My chest felt as if a sledgehammer had hit me. I began sobbing, walking from one room to another back and forth—"No, no, no, no, no," I repeated. I just kept walking; I could not sit. I gasped for air. The shock, the agony for both of us, defies description. The horror was overpowering.

At some point–I don't remember how much time went by--we started trying to contact our son. We called Michelle to see how we could reach David. Unfortunately, we could not talk to him until his work shift ended. He was working on a new aircraft carrier at Newport News Shipyard and could not be reached. We had to wait until he got home.

It had to be a mistake.

Sometime around 5:00 pm, David phoned. His voice was calm, and all he said was that he was sure we were mistaken. We had heard wrong.

I remember hearing grief counselors and psychiatrists on TV talk shows say that when a sudden, unexpected death occurs, you go through stages—one of the first is denial. I had never paid much attention to talk about death and what happens when someone reacts to unexpected death. I brushed it aside. I tended to doubt the psychologists' words—it all sounded like psycho-babble to me. How could anyone deny death? But it's true. I went into denial—we all went into denial. It had not happened; we had heard wrong. For some time, I convinced myself that we had misunderstood. That evening, we would phone Angie to verify that this was all a mistake; some other student had been killed.

David had me convinced. Why wait until the evening to talk to Angie? We would call Joe Dales' office again and clear up this terrible mistake. Janice had heard wrong. It wasn't Angie.

My heart suddenly felt lighter. That was it–a terrible, terrible mistake. What a relief!

I told David I would call Joe's office right back and clear up the whole matter. As soon as I had it cleared up I would call him back. But, it was not a misunderstanding—we had heard correctly. Hearing the words again was like hearing the news for the first time—the pain, the suffocation. I phoned David—no mistake. There was silence on the other end of the line.

Sue Dales' Premonition

On the other side of Virginia, on the morning of January 16, Angie's mother, Sue Dales, woke up with a feeling of dread. For reasons she cannot explain to this day, she didn't want to get dressed; she didn't want to go to work; she just cried and cried. Nothing was wrong that she knew of. She simply had the same ominous feeling she had experienced the day her brother died.

Angie always brought Rebecca to her parents to wait for the school bus. The two would play on the front lawn until the bus arrived, and then Angie would go home to get ready for her law classes. Sue typically would be preparing to go to work, but that morning she simply sat at the kitchen table holding her head.

Angie was surprised to see her mother in such a state and asked her what was wrong. Sue didn't know, but she felt a terrible foreboding. Angie tried to cheer up her mother, then went outside to be with Rebecca until the bus came. Through the windows, Sue could see Angie and Rebecca playing. The two laughed and teased each other. Usually, their happiness and laughter were infectious, but not this morning—she could not break out of the blackness that engulfed her.

Once the bus arrived, Angie returned to the house and asked again what was wrong, "Do you want me to start your car?" Sue thanked her, adding that she would do it herself. Angie turned, went outside, and drove home to prepare for the day's classes.

Sue owned a restaurant in Oakwood, and shortly after Angie left, she headed for work. Something was wrong—all morning, she couldn't keep her mind off Angie. She couldn't concentrate on work, so she decided to go to Angie's house, clean it, and make dinner--a surprise. Angie did not like to cook, so Sue frequently surprised her by preparing the evening meal. With dinner ready and waiting, Angie could spend the evening playing with Rebecca and studying.

The phone rang while Sue was standing on Angie's porch. By the time she got inside, she could hear the last few words of her sister-in-law on the answering machine. She was too late, but she could tell by her sister-in-law's voice that something was wrong. A chill went through her.

When Sue phoned the restaurant back, her sister-in-law said, "Sue, something bad has happened." Sue's first thought was that Danny, Angie's father, had been in an accident—but no, it wasn't that. Was it Rebecca? Had she been hurt at school? No, it was Angie, and Sue needed to get to the hospital.

Danny Learns of the Shooting

Danny Dales had gone to Bluefield to work on his son Joe's house. Danny was very handy and always had a project in the works; he loved working on home improvements. He had been at Joe's for two days. That Wednesday, Danny was in the basement working on the water pipes.

Danny had rheumatoid arthritis, aggravated by years of laboring in a crouching position in coal mines. Physical labor and working with his hands helped ease the pain and kept his mind off the discomfort. That day Joe was home for lunch, and the family had just finished eating when the phone rang. It was approximately 1:45 pm. His aunt Mary was on the line. "Come at once—there has been a shooting at the school."

Joe's first thought was Rebecca, Rebecca's school. "What school?" he blurted out.

"The law school," she said, choking back tears. "Angie has been shot. She's being evacuated to Bristol. Your mother is on her way to pick up Rebecca."

Joe hung up the phone without saying a word.

Trying to remain calm and force back tears, Joe walked to his father's SUV. Danny had gone outside to get some tools out of the vehicle. He was in the back of the SUV, and Joe asked him to get out: he had something important to tell him.

Danny just kept rummaging for tools, ignoring his son as if he knew intuitively the horrible words about to be spoken.

"Dad, I have something important to say," Joe insisted, trying to cover the alarm and anxiety he felt. "There has been a shooting at the law school. Angie has been shot; she's being evacuated to Bristol."

Both men were silent.

Without saying a word, Danny got out of the SUV. According to Joe, the blood had drained from his face. He looked crushed and disoriented when he opened the driver's door, climbed inside, and headed for home.

Joe hurried back into the house. He and his wife Kay threw things into a suitcase if they had to stay in Bristol. They sped off after Danny.

Kay, frantically dialing the cell phone repeatedly, tried to call Aunt Wanda, who worked at Buchanan General Hospital but could not reach her.

Kay then called her mother, who worked at the school board next to the hospital. Her mother confirmed that at least one professor was dead, as well as one student.

Hoping against hope that the student was not Angie, Joe had caught up with his father and passed him. He tried to get his father's attention and flashed him the thumbs-up sign; he was trying to reassure Danny that the one student could not be Angie.

Danny followed at breakneck speed. If Angie had been evacuated to Bristol, they would drive directly there. But when Joe made the right turn at Claypool Hill instead of going to Bristol, Danny's heart sank. Joe was on the cell phone all the way from Bluefield to Claypool Hill and the turn, in Danny's mind, meant something was seriously wrong—Angie had not been taken to Bristol. They stopped at Rebecca's school. Sue had not picked her up. With Rebecca in hand, they sped to the hospital.

Sue was waiting for them. There was no news. No one would tell her anything. All three knew instantly that the worst had happened. For Danny, the worry was unbearable. He didn't remember why, but when he saw Sue's face, he turned and ran out the door and through the parking lot. He ran as fast as he could as if to escape the horror. He said he needed fresh air. He needed to breathe. He was suffocating—he ran, and ran, and ran.

"Quick, Joe, go after your daddy. See where he is going," Sue said. As Joe bolted out the hospital door, Dr. Briggs came up to Sue and callously said, "Your daughter is dead."

"I want to see my daughter."

"No, you don't," Dr. Briggs said in an official cold tone. "She's in the morgue." Dr. Briggs turned and walked away, leaving her standing there. He offered no words of comfort, no show of concern for the dead woman's mother, just a statement of the cold reality. This was the same Dr. Briggs who had rushed to the shooting site minutes after the tragedy, the same Dr. Briggs who had appeared on national television describing Peter Odighizuwa as "a time bomb" waiting to go off, the same Dr. Briggs who erroneously indicated nothing could be done for Angie when he saw her alive and bleeding. He did not—or would not—spend a moment comforting the dead woman's mother.

Moments later, Danny and Joe came back through the front door. Danny didn't know where he was running or what he was doing. He had just needed to run from what he knew was the awful truth.

Sue just shook her head; she could not repeat Dr. Briggs's words. Her mouth was dry. The words would not form on her lips.

Danny leaned against the wall and slowly slid down, staring into space. He had seen his daughter the previous Sunday evening on her birthday. As she left the house, Danny had turned to his Angie and said, "Happy birthday, baby girl. I love you." These were his last words to his precious daughter.

The Law School

The Appalachian School of Law opened in the fall of 1997 on a renovated campus in the center of Grundy. The town had beaten other communities such as Abingdon and Norton to become the school's home. After the demand for coal waned, the region languished in an economic depression for decades. The school was integral in bringing new life to this once prosperous community. The Appalachian School of Law was viewed as the crown jewel of this effort to bring prosperity and opportunity to the entire region.

Great Hope to Revive Grundy

With all her heart and soul, Angie bought into the promise of its promoters that the Appalachian School of Law was the great hope to revive the Grundy area. She wanted to be a part of this dream, this hope for a brighter future.

But, from the outset, the school was a magnet for the region's social elite. According to court documents, "[The school] was often used [as] the primary gathering place of the so-called 'high society' of the community, which included members of the administration, faculty, and board of the law school, many of whom resided in the Grundy community and [the school] was used to elevate their 'social standing.' Members of the faculty often mingled 'socially' with students."

The picture that emerges of the Appalachian School of Law is not of an institution dedicated to bringing good education to talented individuals who might not otherwise have that opportunity but of a school dominated by the community's elite social climbers.

Establishing a new law college in a community with no institutions of higher learning is not easy, but the school that promised so much, and generated so much enthusiasm, was deeply flawed. Perhaps some of these flaws were to be expected. However, some faculty and staff's management had character traits that leave an observer scratching his or her head.

Poor Management Created Problems

The school appears to have been riddled with mismanagement, questionable ethical practices, sexism, and even racism. In hindsight, the magnitude of the problems was so great that it is difficult to explain why no one focused on the need to deal with the problems and provide campus security.

The school apparently had some problems attracting a first-rate staff—not unusual or unexpected for a new college. But, the examples of immature behavior raise serious questions. A very telling example of the staffing problem is found in a lawsuit filed by Professor Steven Cooper in the second year of the school's operation. On October 20, 1998, Steven Cooper filed a suit against the law school "for wrongful discharge brought by a tenured and accomplished professor of law who was unjustly dismissed for cursing at a junior colleague who had rudely questioned his character and honesty."

According to Professor Cooper's lawsuit, he was awarded tenure "effective August 1, 1997, upon the recommendation of [the school's] president, all as evidenced by the letter dated January 17, 1997, from President Lucius F. Ellsworth...." The suit further states that Cooper accepted "the low salary only because he had been assured he would be awarded tenure, i.e., a lifetime employment contract."

The suit then recounts the following events: "On or about April 21, 1998, a professor, Eric Holmes, rudely shouted a string of curse words during a meeting of several members of the law school's staff and faculty. Holmes' foul language included repeated declarations of 'bullshit' and 'horseshit' well within earshot of those in attendance."

Then the suit asserts, "Before walking out of the meeting on April 21, 1998, Holmes approached Cooper from the rear in a threatening manner, shook his finger, and stated loudly 'Shut the fuck up.'"

On May 6, 1998, Cooper allegedly argued with another faculty member, Gail Kintzer, which centered on Kintzer calling Cooper "lazy," impugning his commitment to the law school and its mission, and questioning his request to be reimbursed for school-related expenses. The lawsuit claims that Kintzer complained to Dean Dennis Olson about Cooper cursing at her as well as Holmes cursing at Cooper. Dean Olson subsequently reprimanded both Holmes and Cooper.

The lawsuit then cites a memorandum dated July 15, 1998, in which the chairman of the school board charged that Cooper had violated various rules and laws when he cursed Kintzer. The suit says that on July 23, 1998, the school board voted to suspend Cooper without pay and bar him from the campus. The board did not suspend Holmes. In fact, they promoted him to dean in July 1998 after removing Dean Olson.

In September 1998, Cooper appeared before the school board, expressed regret for cursing Kintzer, and asked to be reinstated. He was not.

Other Unprofessional Conduct

The lawsuit recounts some rather unprofessional conduct by faculty members who are part of a profession that prides itself on intellect, education, and proper use of the English language. The lawsuit puts a cloud over all three attributes that are said to be at the heart of the legal profession and reveals a disturbing facet of the law school faculty's lack of professionalism.

I spent nearly eight years in university training, and since 1987, I have taught college-level writing. Not one time in all those years did I ever encounter educators who stooped to such low levels of conduct and foul language.

Had the above been the only example of the faculty's poor judgment, one could chalk it up to an exception. But, at least one other member of the staff had a reputation for not being able to conduct a class without using a string of four-letter words.

Professor Dale Rubin

Professor Dale Rubin had a reputation for using profane language. According to students in his classes, he would pick on students and unmercifully ridicule them throughout the semester. His conduct made many feel uncomfortable and certainly was not conducive to learning. Despite his education at Stanford and Berkeley and many articles published in learned journals, he appears to have never mastered civility, dignity, or some of the more lofty ideals commensurate with his chosen profession.

Earlier, when the position of Dean of Students had opened, Professor Dale Rubin was one of three candidates for the job. Professor Tony Sutin and Professor Tom Blackwell, the two murdered faculty members, were also candidates. Professor Sutin was awarded the post.

In documents filed with the Wise County Circuit Court, Professor Rubin's own words provide an alarming insight into his character. Reading his words reminds me of what I tell my writing students. "Writing is thinking on paper, and your thoughts are the window to your soul." The court document shows that Rubin could not conceal his anger and frenzy when Sutin received the post. The following are excerpts from Rubin's written account of his reaction.

Racism Acts

A Black Man Reacts
June 2000

> O.K., so I'm the type of nigga that don't take no shit off white folks. That's why I'm writing about this shit in the outback of Grundy, Va. But make no mistake about it, I could be the most effective Uncle Tom in America and I would STILL be writing about this shit…I would just be located on the 56th floor of some high rise in New York.
>
> At least the white folks on the interviewing committee had enough respect to inquire whether I would be disappointed if I did not get the job! …
>
> What is more surprising to me is MY reaction to this latest act of racism in my life. Y'all know that I ain't no shrinking violet. … Well, it's not disappointment, it's anger. I am really fucking pissed off! And why am I pissed off? Well, it's because the white folks have forced me out of my typical way of dealing with racism. …
>
> And I thought about this white boy, who is jewish by the way, who is the openly and unflinchingly proud beneficiary of this fucked up racist decision. The motherfucker should not have even been a candidate! And all this time, I thought jews liked niggas.
>
> So yea, I'm pissed off. I'm angry. I dislike white people. I'm 56 years old and this shit is starting to get to me. And for these reasons, I am momentarily faltering. But you can't feel this way and continue to work with white people. You can't feel this way and live a happy life. So I will bounce back. I will get back into the "what do you expect from those white motherfuckers" mode. You can't think about all the shit I've talked about on a regular basis and maintain your sanity. You have got to let it go.
>
> And sometimes you just have to write about it.

Cutting Corners

In their understandable enthusiasm to become established, it seems that the law school's founders cut corners and danced around the edges of ethical behavior. For example, The Canons of Official Conduct for the State of Virginia includes a statement that "[judges] shall not use or permit the use of the prestige of judicial office for fundraising or membership solicitation." Yet, the school has held, until recently, an annual golf tournament to raise money. It used Judge Nicholas E. Persin's name and the prestige of his office to publicize the contest. Indeed, the tournament was referred to as the "N.E. Persin/Appalachian School of Law Golf Tournament and Gala." Linking Judge Persin's name to a golf tournament may not be an infraction of the law. Still, it is indicative of a willingness by all parties to "bend" the limits of ethical behavior.

Former employees have presented more disturbing indications that the school's administration was willing to cut corners. In one instance, a former employee claims to have been privy to school officials' willingness to "play fast and free" with statistics. The individual claims to have been reading a file containing evidence that the school was willing to "adjust" statistics relating to the school's minority enrollment—specifically to Peter Odighizuwa's status as a student.

A school official met with the employee and told him to destroy the file. The employee made a copy of the file and then followed instructions. That copy was given to the attorneys who filed a lawsuit against the school on behalf of Angela Dales' estate.

The same employee says that he was sent home when insurance investigators were on the campus after the shooting. The school officials told him to stay at home, and he would be paid for his day off. It was best for the employee to stay home, he was told, because the school was sure that the employee "…would not want to do or say something that would hurt the victims' families."

Most people who have read the evidence say that the law school failed to control conditions on the campus, ignored danger signals, and largely dismissed Odighizuwa's aggressive behavior toward faculty, administrative staff, and students. On the rare occasions that the school responded to Odighizuwa, it did so in ineffective ways.

The law school has done the minimum necessary to acknowledge our loss— just enough to make good press and say they have done something.

How Could This Happen in Grundy?

We read about shootings. We read about innocent people being gunned down, and we sympathize with the victims and their families. But, we don't understand the impact murder has on someone until a family member is killed. We cannot find the words to express our feelings or explain to anyone the long road back to some sort of stable mental condition that will allow us to function.

A Small Southwest Virginia Town

How could this happen in Grundy? How could this happen at all? We were to find out "how" as we began the long, difficult road to recovery—a road we have not yet entirely traveled. Along this road, we have found no bravery, courage, or willingness to get at the roots of the evil that led to the tragedy in that small Southwest Virginia town.

Only as the horror began to set in and as we began to rebuild what were once happy lives did we realize how this tragedy could happen in Grundy. Over the months that lay ahead, we would realize just how ripe the Appalachian School of Law, Grundy, the Commonwealth of Virginia, and much of the U.S. was, and is, for tragedies such as the shootings of January 16, 2002.

On the night before Angie's funeral, David and Michelle drove up from Newport News to spend the night with Janice and me. It was a drizzling, bone-chilling January night. We said very little to each other. All four of us were drained of energy and emotions. No one cried; it was a surrealistic situation. When we did talk, the conversation was about everything but the shooting.

The following day we left for Grundy at 5:00 am. The family was to gather at the funeral home that evening an hour before the general viewing. I had talked to Joe, and he asked us to come during the last ten minutes of family time.

Our son, Ben, and his fiancée, Sutopa, flew in from Boston and drove from Washington, DC, with our youngest son, Richard.

For Janice, David, Michelle, and me, the eight-hour trip had been as pleasant as it could be—punctuated by long periods of silence. There were even some light moments. But when we got to Claypool Hill and made the turn toward Grundy, the talking stopped. We were silent for the rest of the trip, all of us dreading the reality that awaited us a few miles down the road. The sky was dark, and the clouds were laden with water.

In a rush, I could hear Angie giving us directions the first time we came to visit. She had the most beautiful soft Virginia accent. It was as if she were next to me saying "turn at Claypool Hill"—saying it as only she could.

That memory is so strong that if there were another way of getting to Grundy, I would use it to avoid hearing her voice. She lies on a hillside facing home and the mountains she loved so dearly. Now, whenever we make the turn, we pass her grave.

The road from Claypool Hill to Grundy traverses some of the most beautiful scenery on earth. When Angie talked about the mountains of Virginia, she radiated love for her home.

An Economically Depressed Community

Heading toward the center of Grundy, one would be overpowered by the gray, economically depressed aspects of the community. Going through the town, one cannot help but notice that Grundy is a community of the few "haves" and many "have-nots." What middle class there once was is now small in number. Despite some revival in coal mining, widespread poverty still plagues the community.

The town was devastated by a major flood in 1977 when the Levisa River spilled over its banks. The central business district never really recovered. With a $24.2 million government grant, part of the downtown area has moved up the mountainside, and the riverbed is being rerouted. The region may not be wealthy in a material sense, but it is rich in pride, hospitality, and the willingness of its citizens to work hard to earn a living. Anyone familiar with the mountain people of western Virginia and West Virginia will vouch for their honesty. The overwhelming majority practice Christian values of fair play and treating others as they want to be treated. Some of the most beautiful, hardworking people live and work in this part of Virginia and throughout Appalachia.

As we arrived in Grundy to begin the arduous task of putting our lives back in order; to seek answers to many of the nagging questions surrounding the shooting, it would soon become apparent that a dichotomy exists between the values of the average Grundy residents and those who hold the reins of economic and political power.

"How could this happen in Grundy?"

We checked into Grundy's one motel. Our other two sons, Richard and Ben, and Ben's fiancée, Sutopa, arrived almost simultaneously. David and I walked to the desk to register. The clerk knew why we were there and repeated, "How could this happen in Grundy? I used to tell people you don't even have to lock your doors here. No more. We can't say that anymore! We give people the opportunity to come to this country, they come here, and this is how they repay us," she continued.

I listened without saying a word. I looked at my six-foot-four-inch strapping son and watched the tears stream down his face.

How could this happen in Grundy? The sad truth is that despite the virtues of most of the region's residents, there is also a twisted sense of logic and fair play from a small but influential group of people.

Grundy still has a high crime rate, and the press reports widespread corruption. Murders go unsolved—suspicious deaths occur in the local jail. Bodies are found, but the crimes are never solved. Read the crime report in the Grundy newspaper: shootings, murders, disappearances.

The Case of Tina Stiltner

A strange Grundy case centers on the death of Tina Stiltner while she was in custody. Ms. Stiltner was taken into custody by the Buchanan County Sheriff's Department at 0900 on 31 January 2002. An officer pulled her over on suspicion of driving while intoxicated. Taken to jail, she was placed in a holding cell just a few feet from the jailer's desk. Ms. Stiltner lost her life that night. No one saw anything, and authorities labeled her death accidental. Yet they answered no questions, and one newspaper publicly stated its belief that she was murdered while in custody.

News of Ms. Stiltner's death gave rise to rumors that she died of a drug overdose. But, an autopsy report showed no traces of drugs in her system. The autopsy report listed the cause of death as strangulation. Furthermore, there is no evidence of any object, such as a rope or cord, which could have contributed to Ms. Stiltner's death. The question remains, how was Ms. Stiltner strangled?

Tina Stiltner left twin sons who entered the third grade in August 2004.

In a preliminary hearing in Abingdon, Virginia May 24, 2004, United States Judge Jones told Tina Stiltner's family that there was insufficient evidence to take the case before a jury. He advised the attorney for the plaintiff to produce more evidence, or he would dismiss the case.

It finally appears that the courts will get to the bottom of Stiltner's death. On August 31, 2006, the former jailer, David Shawn Hicks of Grundy, went on trial for perjury in connection with the Stiltner case. Hicks was indicted in January on five counts of perjury and two counts of obstruction of justice. The press reported that U.S. Attorney John Brownlee charged that Hicks lied under oath to a federal grand jury and lawyers collecting depositions in connection with the investigation.

For us, the question is this: if it takes the courts more than four years to follow up on a case of a mysterious death by strangulation while a person is in custody, can we ever expect answers to our questions about the inappropriate actions at the Appalachian School of Law both before and after Angie's murder? As the Stiltner case unfolded, my concerns grew about our prospects for the legal system to help us because some of the most pressing questions centered on the law school and its actions or inactions.

The Murder Trial

The state spent hundreds of thousands of dollars to assure that Peter Odighizuwa's rights were protected and that he got a fair trial. A major law firm, whose partners oppose the death penalty, came to Odighizuwa's aid. Spending this time and money is how it *should* be in our democracy. A life hangs in the balance—even if it is the life of a murderer. No stone should be left unturned, and no expense spared to ensure a fair trial. But what about the lives of the victims and their families? Neither the state nor the "prominent" law firm representing Peter Odighizuwa did anything to return a seven-year-old orphan's life to some semblance of order.

$100,000 in Attorney Fees

According to some sources, the state paid over $100,000 to the law firm of Turk and Groot for Odighizuwa's defense. But, when Angie's parents wanted copies of the court proceedings, they were charged ten cents a page. As if the loss of their daughter wasn't enough, Buchanan County seemed determined to squeeze every last dime out of the Dales.

Time and time again, before the trial, our questions went unanswered, or promises to get back to us were unfulfilled. Rather than seek the truth, law enforcement officials and the prosecutor in Grundy focused on what was best for the Commonwealth of Virginia and not what was best in pursuit of truth, justice, and the victims' rights.

Perhaps the most disappointing aspect of the ordeal leading up to Peter Odighizuwa's trial was the family's dealings with the Commonwealth's Attorney. On first impression, she exuded sympathy for the Dales' loss, and I'm sure her expressions of sympathy were sincere. But, having compassion for a murder victim's family and being disingenuous are not mutually exclusive.

Death Penalty off the Table

The Commonwealth's Attorney repeatedly assured the Dales that she was going for the death penalty, but she did not. Indeed, from the outset, the Dales were strongly pushing for the death penalty. However, Dean Sutin's and Professor Blackwell's families (and possibly the law school) wanted a life sentence. In meetings with the Commonwealth's Attorney, Angie's parents had the distinct impression that they were being asked to go along with agreements that had already been reached. After repeated assurances that the death penalty would be pursued in the final analysis, the Dales were called in and told a deal had been struck for life in prison.

In the twenty years since the shooting, the answer emerging from the mountains of red tape, legal mumbo-jumbo, stonewalling, and silence is that victims' families have few rights to answers. How can the average citizen believe "in the system?" If "what is best for the Old Dominion" is put ahead of the needs of its citizens, how can the average citizen believe in "rule by law?"

Grundy Mirrors what Happens throughout America

Angie's tragic death and the legal machinations surrounding her murder, the willingness of law enforcement officials and commonwealth's attorneys to play fast and free with the emotions of victims' families goes far beyond the bounds of decency. The sobering truth is that what happened in Grundy after the shooting may not be different from today's events throughout the country.

One reason the media may have wanted to avoid delving into the murders of Angela Dales, Professor Blackwell, and Dean Sutin may be that it would force them to ask some basic questions like "How can a man known by the courts to abuse his wife still get his hands on a gun?" Such a question might jolt readers and listeners out of their complacency and offend powerful interests. Just to ask the question rouses an irrational response from otherwise well-educated, well-balanced individuals. When I queried a member of my family, he immediately fell back on such platitudes as, "We can't restrict hunters from their right to hunt." What does hunting have to do with a school shooting? Many hunters have children, and if you were to ask them, I'm sure these hunters would say, "Yes, keep guns out of the hands of the mentally ill and emotionally unstable. Keep guns out of the hands of spouse abusers."

The media, particularly in Virginia, won't raise this question even in the most circumspect way. They back away from addressing whether there is any merit to restricting access to guns—even for individuals with a history of domestic violence and public aggression. More upsetting is that to utter such a question would threaten one of the most powerful lobbies in this country—the NRA.

Gun Control in Virginia

On those rare occasions when Virginia's media raises the subject of restrictions on gun ownership, they choose their words carefully. They use words that stop short of causing readers to ask whether something is wrong with their reasoning or values related to violence and the use of firearms. Reporters miss an opportunity to educate the public by suggesting that they might need to rethink a flawed bias. The deceitful aspect of this word parsing is that it gives Virginia's citizens a false sense of security.

When it comes to guns, logic collides with bias and emotions—and logic loses. This fact has always puzzled me. In his book, *The Thinkers' Toolkit*, Morgan Jones points out that "most [humans] earn a failing grade in elementary logic.... We're not just frequently incompetent [in thinking logically]. We're also willfully and skillfully illogical."

Jones adds, "Compelling research on cognitive psychology has shown that we are logical only in a superficial sense; at a deeper level, we are systematically illogical and biased." I would go a step further and say that humans not only prefer the emotional gratification of biases, but many are anti-intellectual to the point of being dishonest and, in some cases, paranoid. The paranoia of some is frightening. This element of society advocates unrestricted access to weapons—even if it means giving the mentally ill and unstable the right to bear arms. And, when this paranoia reaches the Christian pulpit, it is even more alarming. I want to ask—would Jesus have carried a gun?

The bias that prevents laws restricting unstable and dangerous individuals from owning guns is, in fact, a prejudice of individuals who are either unwilling or unsuited to deal with the real world. It has prevented laws from being considered, much less passed, to block individuals with ties to or sympathy for terrorist groups from buying weapons.

Challenging a Flawed Bias

There is only one way to change a flawed bias once it has taken root: exposing ourselves to new information and objectively weighing that evidence against our mindset. If we have only half-truths and fragmentary evidence and are not exposed to all sides of the argument, we come up with conclusions that make us feel comfortable in our prejudices. We fall prey to sound bites and clever wordplay. The sad truth is that most of us accept sugar-coated words to avoid an uncomfortable truth.

The choice of words—the need to be ethical in what you say and write and the need for accuracy—recently came up in a course I was teaching. It was an analytical writing course for a member of the Intelligence Community. To my dismay, one young intelligence analyst (a lawyer) said that she could not use the word "genocide" in official publications to describe the widespread killings in Bosnia. The reason given was international law. To call the execution of thousands of innocent civilians "genocide" in official U.S. publications would trigger some aspect of a UN resolution. She explained that under international law, if the term "genocide" is used, the UN and its member states must take action to stop it. I have no problem with that. Isn't that why we signed the treaty?

Furthermore, members of the Intelligence Community present their analyses to policymakers; they do not set or make policy. Anytime you prevent members of the Intelligence Community from using the correct word to describe a situation, you do a disservice to our elected officials and the American public.

Instead, the U.S. government and the news media called what was happening in Bosnia "ethnic cleansing." There are examples in history of "ethnic cleansing"—where a group of people is forcibly moved from one area to another without loss of life. The situation in Bosnia was not "ethnic cleansing." It was genocide. A lack of precision in language describing an atrocity undercuts the idea of getting at the truth. Yet, this type of word game is what lawyers and reporters are forcing on us—whether it involves the murder of Angela Dales or the mass murder of thousands of Muslims in Bosnia.

Ignoring Mass Murder

If the U.S. government—at the highest level—will not call examples of mass murder by the correct name genocide, then we should not be surprised that officials in Grundy are willing to obfuscate. Have we been living in a dream world, a world of illusions? Is this the democracy and rule by law we are bringing to Iraq? Have over 3,000 young Americans died and another 20,000 been wounded in Iraq to make the world safe for this type of political-legal system? Where is the truth? This form of "truth avoidance" in Grundy and throughout American society appears to be part of a wholesale effort to sugar-coat everything unpleasant. No matter how someone plays with words, what happened in Bosnia was genocide on a scale not seen since Nazi Germany. What happened in Grundy resulted from people in positions of authority not taking the necessary steps to avoid the shooting tragedy.

In my family's quest for answers, examinations of Virginia laws and discussions with attorneys have left us bewildered. Angie wanted so badly to be a legal professional—she held it in high regard. She would have fought for abused wives; she would have fought for every child victim of the system. Now, her child waits for answers from the Virginia legal profession.

When the family of a murder victim asks for answers, legal luminaries rub their chins, check their golf handicaps, and ponder what, if anything, they will say. Angie wanted to work in family law to uphold the values she held dear. Ironically, the injustice she intended to combat has hampered her family's efforts to get at the truth.

God's Will

If our search for truth through legal means has been sobering and disappointing, our search for answers and comfort in religion has been horrifying.

Proclaimed Christian members of our family, who never let a meal go by without a prayer, are pillars of the church, ranting and raving over the evils of alcohol, have simply ignored Angie's death. They ignored the screams of a small child when told her mother was gunned down. They continue to behave as if the shooting never happened.

To these individuals, drinking alcohol is a sin, but murdering someone— well, "God has a reason for all things; it must have been the victim's time." How do these so-called Christians deal with Angie's murder? With silence. If you cannot deal with senseless acts of violence—if you cannot fit the cruel, violent death of an innocent young woman into your religious philosophy— just ignore it, ignore the whole problem. Even when it is a family member— just ignore it.

One family member couldn't wait to tell us that if two law school students had not carried guns in their cars, Peter Odighizuwa would not have been overcome so quickly. How incredibly insensitive and untrue. Eye witness accounts consistently state that Odighizuwa had been subdued before the students—with their guns—appeared on the scene.

Even if the students with guns had played a critical role in subduing Odighizuwa, the fact remains that an unbalanced individual with a documented history of violence was allowed to buy a gun and kill three innocent people, wounding three others. This fact didn't seem to count. Yet, there are individuals in our own family who have used this tragedy for their political ends. Maybe it just didn't register.

The mixing of religion and guns even defiled Angie's funeral. The minister showed little respect for the family by turning his sermon into NRA propaganda. He quoted directly from the NRA mantra saying, "Guns don't kill people, people kill people." In fact, guns *do* kill people mainly when the law does not prevent spouse abusers and the mentally unbalanced from owning guns. Not only did his words upset members of an already distraught family, but then he added insult to injury by chewing gum and rocking back and forth with an inappropriate grin on his face. He appeared to even gloat over his accomplishment. He was proud to have slipped an NRA commercial into his sermon.

No Legal Recourse in Virginia School Shootings

Incidents of students taking weapons to school are no longer uncommon. In Virginia, if a shooting occurs on public school grounds, and even if the school authorities are negligent—the victims and their families have little or no legal recourse against the school. Seeking redress against a state or public institution—even when gross negligence can be proven—is considered frivolous by some lawmakers in Richmond. The doctrine of sovereign immunity generally protects public schools (and other public institutions). This doctrine shields taxpayer-funded institutions from many lawsuits. More often than not, the courts seem to extend this doctrine to private companies and organizations in Virginia.

The Virginia Supreme Court appears reluctant to make any ruling that holds a private or public organization responsible for the actions of employees or students, even when those individuals have a record of violence that is well known to the organization or company that hired the individual.

The more I investigate what the legal profession has done to chip away at an individual's rights, the more dismayed and frightened I become. All the views I held about a fair system have disappeared. The emerging picture is not devotion to the average citizen's rights but to an agenda and bias. In the case of premises liability and the law, the prejudice is to protect—at all costs—private businesses and public organizations. The law in Virginia says that even if a man beats or threatens to harm or kill his spouse and children and that spouse gets a restraining order against him; he can still buy a gun and bullets. In the Old Dominion, a man such as Peter Odighizuwa can beat his wife, have a record of violence, and still buy a gun.

Odighizuwa Protection Order

In the case of Peter Odighizuwa, the Emergency Protection Order that his wife filed against him lasted for one week. Mrs. Odighizuwa never took the next step to get a Restraining Order. Even if she had, it would not have prevented him from owning or buying a weapon. In Virginia, Odighizuwa—a man with a long and widespread history of violence, a man whom a psychiatrist described as a "time bomb waiting to go off"—was free to buy all the weapons he wanted.

If you were a Martian and landed in Richmond, you would assume that not only does everyone have the right to own a gun, but they can legally turn that weapon on anyone for any reason.

In other states, that is not the case. Virginia wraps itself in the flag, patriotism, and religion but appears to rank the safety of its residents and their children a distant second to the right to own a gun.

When Odighizuwa killed Angie, a close friend wondered how soon it would be before someone she knew or a family member of someone she knew would be gunned down. What a terrible commentary on our society!

While I was teaching a course for Intelligence officers, a student came in frustrated and said a trucker had tailgated him so closely that he felt like pulling out his pistol and shooting the truck tires. Incredible! We seem to believe, as a nation, as a people, that owning and using a gun is the answer to our problems.

Our legal system ignores victims' rights, but gun lobbies spend millions to ensure that individual Americans can be better armed than some small countries.

The First Anniversary

Christmas 2002 was somber and New Year's worse. We did not put up the tree, nor was there the toy train for Rebecca. Only the candles shone in the windows, indicating that there might be a holiday at hand. Angie's parents and Rebecca stayed in Grundy, and we went to our youngest son's home in Manassas.

Commonwealth Attorney Sheila Tolliver

As the first anniversary of the shooting approached, we decided to take up the Commonwealth's Attorney, Sheila Tolliver, on her offer to meet with us. She agreed to help answer the Dales' questions. Angie's father was distraught because no one had ever taken the time to share some of the details that would mean so much to the family. Who took Angie to the hospital? Where did she die? No one told him then, and no one told him in subsequent meetings.

However, our expectations of getting long-sought answers to questions proved unfounded. In this instance, as in many others, we had allowed our hope to soar. Even allowing for the limitations of human mental processes and the problems inherent in a crime scene investigation, what took place during the meeting was alarming in terms of uncovering shortcomings in the criminal investigative procedures associated with the law school shootings.

Arrogance and Unfounded Disrespect

Ms. Tolliver arranged a meeting with the state highway patrolmen who had responded to the shooting. Angie's parents and brother wanted Janice and me to be present. We agreed to schedule the meeting when we would all be in Grundy for the first anniversary of Angie's death.

Three state highway patrolmen came: John Santolla, Walt Parker, and Ashley Hagy. What ensued was incredible and inexplicable. To this day, I am not sure what was going on. The only explanation I have is that it was an example of "good cop, bad cop" playing a game with the murder victim's family. I am puzzled; I am amazed; I am astounded. I could kick myself for falling prey to such a cheap trick and allowing the officers to get away with such disrespect for the family.

The meeting went from bad to worse. Officer Santolla came in with a box of files on the case and offered to answer any questions. However, the numbers of clear and concise answers were few and far between. The three police officers were unable or unwilling to produce something as simple as a timeline. One of the essential tools used in crime analysis is the construction of the timetable— think "Law Enforcement 101." The true horror of what we had gone through was compounded by a lack of sound investigative practices at the crime scene.

Officer Parker

Officer Parker challenged why he was there, and why any of them were there. From the moment he entered the room, it was apparent that his idea of answering questions that he found distasteful involved the use of verbal abuse or sarcasm. Any sort of discourse requiring logic, reason, and thoughtful response appeared to be alien to him. Only because the Commonwealth's Attorney was sitting there, did the officer's abusive behavior have some limitations, preventing brute force.

Officer Parker appeared to take an instant dislike to me. In response to a point I made, he sarcastically said that if we knew so much, why were the officers there? Then in what hinted at a man who had something to hide or one who had a complete lack of sympathy for crime victims—or maybe both—he lashed out at our "lawsuit." It was an odd assertion because, at that time, there was no lawsuit. We had met with attorneys and discussed the possibility but had gone no further than discussing it. We had not retained an attorney. Instead, we were on a fact-finding quest to determine if we needed legal counsel.

If an investigating police officer cannot get his facts straight in a relatively simple meeting with the family of a shooting victim, what must his "official" reports be like? Officer Parker undercut his credentials as a state highway patrolman, a crime scene investigator, and a human being at every turn. If a police officer is so emotionally strung out that he cannot cope with a murder victim's family, how can we believe anything he says about his investigation of the crime scene?

Officer Parker's credibility went from bad to worse. It turns out that he did not arrive at the crime scene until approximately an hour after the shooting. Yet, he did not hesitate to state what happened emphatically. Often, he was corrected by Officer Santolla, who had arrived at the school four or five minutes after the shooting. I began to wonder why Officer Parker was there at all.

The reality of what we faced began to sink in—and it was suffocating. Was Officer Parker a plant? What was his motive? He appeared to have one overriding motivation—to discourage the Dales from taking legal action. As I recalled that Angie had joked about incompetence in Grundy, a chill passed through me. I realized we might be looking at the face of all she had talked about.

The Commonwealth's Attorney just sat and watched as Officer Parker continued to run amok. The expression on her face was like a deer caught in headlights. Throughout the meeting, Officer Parker's words and actions indicated an unprecedented display of contempt for us. The Commonwealth Attorney's inability to take charge of the meeting and bring the errant officer back in line began to raise serious doubts in my mind, not only about her sincerity but also about her ability to prosecute a major murder trial. The third officer, Officer Hagy, said nothing throughout the meeting—he simply sat and nervously tapped his feet.

Confirmation that Angie was Targeted

The "good cop," Officer Santolla, confirmed our suspicions that Peter Odighizuwa had targeted Angie specifically. Witnesses corroborate this account. Officer Santolla theorized that the killer was headed for the library after shooting the two faculty members. Still, when he got to the student lounge, he saw Angie sitting across the room. Odighizuwa walked around many students, straight up to Angie and fired his pistol hitting her three times. He then turned his gun on two other female students sitting with Angie, wounding both but not killing them.

Why Angie? The only glimpse we have into Odighizuwa's motive for targeting her is a comment he reportedly made that since leaving the school's staff and becoming a student, "Angie was not nice to me."

No one present could answer the question of who transported Angie to the hospital—we are still waiting for someone to tell us.

Officer Santolla confirmed that a Medevac helicopter landed on the school grounds shortly after the shooting. Still, none of the officers would tell us whom they evacuated first or who decided in what order they would remove the victims from the crime scene.

The doctors we consulted in the aftermath of the tragedy told us that triage procedures dictate that the most seriously wounded are evacuated first in the event of a disaster. Angie's injuries were the most serious. Given her gunshot wounds, she should have been treated first. Because no vital organs were hit, Angie would have had a chance if she had been evacuated to the hospital. She bled to death because she did not receive medical attention. The helicopter was there, and the hospital was near. None of the officers would give us any information on who made the evacuation decisions.

We did, however, learn that Dr. Sagan was at the shooting site within minutes of the first reports. He has now left Grundy. It seems that no one bothered to ask him about his triage procedures. As far as we know, no one bothered to ask him if he saw Angie and, if he did, why he didn't get help for her that might have saved her life.

Odighizuwa and Domestic Violence

One issue that bothered all of us was Peter Odighizuwa's domestic violence history. Our question was how someone with a restraining order against him could have a gun. As we were to learn, it was not a restraining order. Mrs. Odighizuwa had an Emergency Protection Order (EPO) against her husband. An EPO, as described to us, is a three-day cooling-off period that does not carry the restrictions of a restraining order. At the end of the three days, Mrs. Odighizuwa had the right to get a restraining order, but she didn't. The whole question was moot.

What isn't moot is that in Virginia, a man can threaten to kill his wife and family, an Emergency Protection Order or a Restraining Order can be placed against him, and he can go right out and buy a gun and bullets. There is no provision in Virginia statutes to search and seize weapons in the home of a man or woman whom the law has deemed a threat to others. There are, however, strict rules for off-color jokes in the workplace. A man or woman can lose his or her job for an off-color remark! In Virginia, touching someone "inappropriately" causes you to lose your job, but beating your spouse and then buying a weapon is okay.

Threatening Email

We then asked the officers about a threatening email message Angie had received over a year before her death. They said they were aware of it and asserted that while they did not know who sent it, the email had nothing to do with Angie's death. The question that bothers us is, if you don't know who sent the message, how can you say with such certainty that it had nothing to do with the shooting? It was equally puzzling that the Commonwealth's Attorney bought this assertion.

As far as we can put the pieces together, this is what happened: Angie's computer accidentally sent a virus to another student's computer. The virus destroyed some or all of the student's files, and he sent the threat. She told her family about the email threat but refused to show it to them. Upon a friend's urging, she did report it to the police and the school.

The threatening email read:

> *You fucking cocksucker. If you ever try to send me another virus again, I will track you down, cut your nipples off, and stick jumper cables in you and connect them to my truck. I'm not bullshittin. Maybe the sheriff will find you hanging from a tree in Longbottom.*

It is against the law to send threats via the internet. An investigation took place, but "nothing" turned up. Ms. Tolliver arranged for us to talk with the investigating officer, Don Lambert.

Ms. Tolliver got Officer Don Lambert on a conference call in her private office. Joe Dales, Ms. Tolliver, and I went into the office for the call. Officer Lambert said he took over the investigation from Officer Whitmore, who had left the state police for a federal job. Lambert was unclear when he assumed the investigation and could not remember who filed the complaint or whether the school was aware and following up on it. He "thought" the school had made at least one inquiry about the investigation but said he couldn't be sure.

Incomplete Investigation

To my request to see the police report of the investigation, Lambert responded by saying he could not give it to me or any member of the family because it was "confidential." He did volunteer to retrieve the report from Richmond, call me, and answer any questions I might have. I am still waiting for that phone call.

Officer Lambert said that his predecessor had gone to the internet provider and tracked down the PC that sent the email. To the best of his memory, the computer belonged to another student, not Peter Odighizuwa. Officer Lambert volunteered that police had questioned the student, who denied any knowledge of the email.

There would have been only one way to verify where the threat came from, and that was from the internet provider. Neither officer Whitmore nor Lambert got the court order, and after sixty days, an internet provider automatically erases all email traffic. That internet provider now says there is no way to retrieve the information. As a result, the state police claim they cannot identify who sent the email to Angie. We continued to ask the police: if you cannot identify the sender of the email, then how can you say beyond a shadow of a doubt that it does not factor into the shooting?

Punishment in the Hereafter?

When I got up to leave the conference call and return to the room where Angie's parents were sitting, I heard officers Parker and Santolla trying to comfort the Dales. They implied that the Dales should be content with the knowledge that Peter Odighizuwa would get his punishment in the hereafter.

Sue Dales was furious. After the meeting, Sue said she could hardly contain her anger, especially at Officer Parker. To this day, her anger boils over when she remembers Parker's behavior. All of us could not help but think: what hypocrites! In other words, the two highway patrolmen were saying, "If you are thinking of a civil lawsuit, why don't you drop it?" In effect, they were patting the Dales on their heads and saying, "There, there, be good. Don't say anything; don't question anything. Now run along home."

We did "run along home" because they answered none of our questions. The only thing the meeting settled was our determination to get to the truth. It was a turning point for us, leaving no doubt that we would hire an attorney; there would be a lawsuit. We would do whatever needed to be done to find the answers.

Jerry Kilgore

The silence related to the threatening email remains deafening. Frustrated and angered and acting on behalf of Angie's parents, I turned to Virginia Attorney General Jerry Kilgore. But, once again, double-speak returned—more sophisticated, but double-speak nevertheless.

Following the shootings, Attorney General Kilgore released the following statement:

> *It was with great sadness that I learned of the shootings that injured and killed innocent people at the Appalachian School of Law in Grundy, Virginia.*
>
> *As natives of Southwest Virginia, my wife Marty and I extend our sympathies to the families and friends who lost loved ones in the senseless act.*
>
> *At the same time we experience these emotions, however, there is a clear sense among us all that as Virginians we cannot tolerate such acts of violence.*
>
> *Our institutions of higher learning are intended to be sanctuaries of education and self-improvement-not places of violence. Law-abiding Virginians may rest assured that law enforcement authorities will identify whoever is responsible and our court system will see that justice is done.*

On July 14, 2004, after nearly a year-and-a-half of waiting for Officer Lambert to answer our questions about the threatening email, I decided to take the Attorney General at his word. I wrote Attorney General Kilgore asking for his assistance.

> *Sir:*
>
> *On January 16, 2002, Angela Dales—the mother of my granddaughter—was shot and killed at the Appalachian School of Law. Nearly a year before the tragedy, she received a threatening email. State Highway Patrolman Lambert, who investigated the email, told the Dales and Cariens families that the police do not know who sent the email but that there is no link between the email and the shooting. Mr. Lambert said we could not see the police report because it is "confidential" but that he would retrieve the report from the Richmond archives and answer any questions we have. This was never done.*
>
> *We are asking the help of your office to:*
>
> * *Explain why the police assert that there is no connection between the email and the shooting when they do not know who wrote it.*
> * *Explain the justification for classifying the police request as 'confidential.'*
> * *Explain the procedures we would have to take to get access to the police report.*
> * *Explain why officer Lambert never followed up on his promise to answer our questions.*
> * *I am enclosing both a copy of the email and a copy of a notarized note authorizing me to act on behalf of Angela Dales' parents—Sue and Danny Dales.*
>
> *I look forward to hearing from you or a member of your staff.*
>
> *David Cariens, Jr.*

In response to my letter, James O. Towey, the Assistant Attorney General for the Commonwealth of Virginia, responded on August 14, 2004:

> *Dear Mr. Cariens,*
>
> *This office is in receipt of your letter with regard to the questions you have concerning the State Police investigation of [a] threatening email received by Angela Dales, the mother of your granddaughter. I am very sorry to hear that Angela's life was subsequently taken at the Appalachian School of Law.*
>
> *I understand from your letter that you have been informed by the investigating officer that the author of the email is not known but there*

is no link between the email and the shooting. Please understand that the authority and jurisdiction of this Office are limited by statute. The Attorney General's Office functions primarily as a law firm for state government. In this capacity, it advises state officials and represents the various state agencies and departments.

Because this Office is not typically charged with the oversight of the investigatory functions of police and local prosecutors, it has no knowledge of the investigation of which you inquire. The proper functioning of our criminal justice system, however, necessitates that criminal investigations be kept confidential. This need is recognized in the Virginia Freedom of Information Act ("VFOIA"), which excludes from its provisions, subject to the discretion of the custodian, "complaints, memoranda, correspondence and evidence relating to a criminal investigation or prosecution, other than criminal incident information."

"Criminal incident information" consists of "a general description of the criminal activity reported, the date and general location the alleged crime was committed, the identity of the investigating officer, and a general description of any injuries suffered or property damaged or stolen." Please note that, under certain circumstances, even "criminal incident information" may be withheld under the VFOIA. Information on obtaining records from the State Police under the VFOIA is contained on their website at www.vsp.state.va.us.

If you are dissatisfied with the manner in which the investigation was handled, or by the fact that the investigating officer did not follow up on his promise to answer your questions, you may file a complaint at any State Police Office or by calling the Internal Affairs Section at telephone number (804) 323-2383. Information on filing complaints can also be obtained at www.vsp.state.va.us/professionalstandards.htm.

Please understand this Office is prohibited from providing legal advice to private citizens and, consequently, nothing herein may be construed as such. You are of course, free to consult with any attorney engaged in private practice of law. I hope you will find this information helpful in obtaining answers to your questions. Thank you for expressing your concerns.

James O. Towey , Assistant Attorney General

The response from the Attorney General's office, albeit polite, contains prime examples of the "double talk" that victims and their families encounter in Virginia. First, Mr. Towey completely ignored the illogical aspect of the police, saying they don't know who wrote the email, but there is no connection to the law school murders. Second, Mr. Towey wrote that his office "is not typically charged with the oversight of local police and local prosecutors' investigatory functions; it has no knowledge of the investigation of which you inquire." The word "typical" tells me that the Attorney General's office *does* have the statutory power to review local investigations. I cannot find anything in the statutes governing the functioning of the Attorney General's office that prohibits him from investigating the circumstances surrounding the email message.

Furthermore, the shootings at the Appalachian School of Law were not typical. The shootings were the worst to occur on school grounds in the state's history up to that time. Suppose there are indications of incompetence in the criminal investigation or in prosecuting the case against the killer. Are we to believe it is "typical" for the Attorney General to turn a blind eye to a miscarriage of justice?

Kilgore Turns his Back on Investigation

A month after the shooting, then-Attorney General Kilgore joined other elected officials in visiting the campus to express condolences. He is quoted as saying, "There is no greater memorial [to the murder victims] than the continued growth and success of this law school." There would be no greater memorial to them and Angela Dales specifically than to uncover all the facts surrounding the tragedy.

The bottom line is that based on the information we have to date, Attorney General Kilgore's office turned its back on delving further into the shooting. I'm convinced that Mr. Kilgore and his staff believed the case would go away if they ignored evidence that might be part of a criminal investigation. They must have thought that we, Angie's family, would go away. We will not go away.

Mr. Towey wrote, "The Attorney General's office functions as a law firm for state government. In this capacity, it advises state officials (I assume the state highway patrol falls in this category) and represents the various state agencies and departments." Isn't it logical to believe that when confronted with evidence or information of questionable police investigations and sloppiness that may have contributed to the state's worst school shooting, the Attorney General's office would "advise" the state police to review their investigation of the case?

Who are the Kilgores?

On the other hand, if I were the attorney general and wanted to run for governor of Virginia, I might look for every way possible to avoid an investigation that would embarrass Virginia officials. If I were the attorney general and part of my political power base was in Southwest Virginia, would I want to alienate the power structure that helped me get where I am today and play a role in my bid for governor? On the other hand, if I were the attorney general and wanted to run for governor of Virginia, I might look for every way possible to avoid an investigation that would embarrass Virginia officials. Kilgore's family members are high rollers in the Republican Party, and he is tied directly to Grundy. His twin brother, Terry Kilgore, was named Dean of Grundy's University of Appalachia's new College of Pharmacy in April 2006. The same power structure that established the Appalachian School of Law is behind the new College of Pharmacy.

Indeed, the Kilgores are such a powerful family that *Richmond Times-Dispatch* reporter Jeff Schapiro ran an article on them on February 11, 2007. Schapiro pointed out that Terry Kilgore's mother is the registrar for Scott County and his father, John, runs the local Republican committee. According to Schapiro, twin brother Terry is the number three Republican in Virginia's House of Delegates and has fifty-seven votes in his pocket.

Looking at the power behind Jerry Kilgore's throne, Schapiro wrote the following:

> *These are the repro [sic] men, whose lobbyists include Ken Hutcheson, manager of Jerry's '05 race against Tim Kaine. They put Terry behind the wheel of a bill extending to them the same supposedly rapacious privileges as their tarted-up kin, payday lenders. Their lead lobbyist, by the way, is one of Jerry's partners, the poker-faced Reggie Jones. Another is Chris Nolen, Jerry's consigliere in the AG's office.*
>
> *Like Jerry's gubernatorial ambitions, the car-title proposal crashed and burned. It was a rare setback for Terry. But not before he collected $4,500 from subprime-market lenders for a 2007 campaign that is likely to be a breeze. This means Terry, who already has raised $107,000, could have extra jack with which to keep friends and make new ones.*
>
> *Terry already has a lot of them. Not all are elected by the people.*
>
> *One is Circuit Judge Teresa Chafin. She is a member of the State Judicial Council, an important advisory group for the black-robed set. Chafin also serves on the Commission on Virginia Courts in the 21st Century, created by Supreme Court Chief Justice Leroy Hassell to recommend ways to modernize the state judiciary.*
>
> *Chafin sits in the 29th Judicial Circuit, which includes Russell County, where she lives. However, her lawyer-husband, Frank Kilgore, who shares*

a name with the political clan but not a bloodline, wants to build on the Clinch River in Wise County. (Frank Kilgore is the chairman of the Appalachian School of Law's Board of Trustees.) That's in the 30th Judicial Circuit.

Problem is, judges are required by law to live in their circuit. Problem solved—almost—by Terry Kilgore.

He proposed adding 28 words to the law: 'However, this residency shall not apply to any sitting judge who resides within the Commonwealth of Virginia upon property that is located contiguous to his respective circuit.

For Chafin and Frank Kilgore, an ex-Democrat and avid environmentalist who's given the Brothers Kilgore $25,067, that literally means land hard by the Wise side of the Russell line.

I asked Frank Kilgore about it, he testily demanded I identify my source. After firing off a couple of emails that were little more than screeds, Kilgore finally said he'd ask Terry to introduce the measure.

Nine days ago, Terry Kilgore quietly yanked that ol' bill–bada bing— killing it for the year. He said he worried it would have a disruptive effect statewide.

Or did Terry Kilgore fear being found out?

After all, he is running a family business.

Terry Kilgore has been a member of the Virginia House of Delegates since 1994. He was there when his brother was Attorney General and when the shootings took place at the law school.

Everywhere we turn, we are confronted with statements citing the limitations of this or that office. We are told that this or that is best for the Commonwealth. The overall picture that emerges is one of a giant shell game. State officials hide behind technicalities, parsing words to justify their inaction.

On the other hand, the Attorney General's office implied we might get access to the information under the Virginia Freedom of Information Act. I decided to follow the Attorney General's advice.

On January 27, 2005, I sent the following letter to the State Police at Wytheville, Virginia:

Sgt. Michael Conroy
State Highway Patrol
P.O. Box 537
Wytheville, Va. 24382
Sgt. Conroy:
This letter is a request to release all records relating to an investigation

of a threatening email sent to Angela Dales on 13 February 2001. A copy of that email is enclosed. Angela Dales was subsequently murdered at the Appalachian School of Law on 16 January 2002.

The investigating officers were David Hale and Patrolman Lambert. In a phone conversation from the Commonwealth Attorney's office in Grundy, Patrolman Lambert offered to retrieve the investigation from the archives in Richmond and answer any of our questions. That promise was never fulfilled.

We are now formally asking, under the Virginia Freedom of Information Act, for access to all documents relating to the investigation of the threatening email.

David Cariens, Jr.

On February 4, I received the following response:

Dear Mr. Cariens:

The Virginia Department of State Police received your request dated January 27, 2005 on January 31, 2005, for a copy of all records relating to an investigation of a threatening email sent to Angela Dales on February 13, 2001.

Please be advised that any files or documents that may be in existence are exempt from mandatory disclosure pursuant to Virginia Code Section 2.2-3706(F) (1), and it is the Department's policy not to release any criminal investigative records.

If you have any questions, please feel free to contact Legal Specialist Sara Poole at (804) 674-2056.

Captain G. Jason Miles, Division Commander
Bureau of Criminal Investigation
P.O. Box 537, Wytheville, Va. 24382

I thought I might have found the elusive key to open the door to the truth about the threats Angie had received. I was wrong: another stonewall, another bureaucratic roadblock. Two things struck me about Captain Miles' letter. First, he raised doubt about whether any documents "may be in existence." Have the documents already been "lost?" Problems surrounding document retention and record-keeping seem to be of epidemic proportions in Virginia—what other conclusion can one come to? Second, Captain Miles said it is policy not to release documents. In other words, there is no law preventing him from releasing documents about the worst school shooting in Virginia and one of the worst this country has ever seen, but "policy" prevents it.

Unanswered Questions

The unanswered questions regarding the school, the police, and the legal establishment only deepened our wounds and crippled our ability to move forward.

The disturbing truth is that even the most straightforward questions went without answers. Parents do have a right to the answers. However, no one in Grundy seems to know them, not the commonwealth's attorney and not the police.

Some ten months before the threatening email was sent, the Virginia legislature passed an amendment to the state's legal code, making it a crime to harass using a computer. They approved it on April 9, 2000—before the email was sent. The State Highway Patrol and the Appalachian School of Law should have known that the threat violated both state and federal laws. Angie received the email on February 13, 2001. The Act to Amend the Code of Virginia reads as follows:

> CHAPTER 849
> An Act to amend the Code of Virginia by adding in Article 7.1 of Chapter 5 of Title 18.2 a section numbered18.2-152.7:1, relating to harassment by computer; penalty.
> [H 1524]
> Approved April 9, 2000
> Be it enacted by the General Assembly of Virginia:
> 1. That the Code of Virginia is amended by adding in Article 7.1 of Chapter 5 of Title 18.2 a section numbered 18.2-152.7:1 as follows:
> Harassment by computer, penalty.
> If any person, with the intent to coerce, intimidate, or harass any person, shall use a computer or computer network to communicate obscene, vulgar, profane, lewd, lascivious, or indecent language, or make any suggestion or proposal of an obscene nature, or threaten any illegal or immoral act, he shall be guilty of a Class I misdemeanor.

Laws Regarding Threatening Emails Ignored

There are federal laws that make sending threatening emails a crime. For example, a federal jury in Tacoma, Washington, convicted Carl Johnson of sending emails and posting essays threatening the lives of Microsoft's founder and chief, Bill Gates, and several government officials. Johnson offered money to anyone who would kill specifically named individuals. The court ruled that

Johnson went too far with his threats and that the threats were not protected under the First Amendment.

Angela Dales's threatening email clearly violated state and federal laws, but she was not Bill Gates. She did not have money, power, or national prestige. If she had had any of those factors, I am sure the threatening email would not have been brushed aside.

The email content alone should have prompted both the school and the police to hunt down its author! Laws covering the abuse of computers date back to the early 1980s in Virginia ("The Virginia Computer Crimes Act" 1984). It is hard to believe that either the law school or law enforcement officials were unaware of such statutes.

If the email had been sent to Lucius Ellsworth, the school's president, I'm sure the police would have made a thorough investigation and left no stone unturned until they identified and punished the sender.

In the months that followed my phone conversation with Officer Lambert, I learned that most schools—nationwide—have policies and/or rules dealing with the abuse of electronic mail.

Marshall University, named after the first Chief Justice of the Supreme Court and located in neighboring West Virginia, adopted an official policy in November 1999 clarifying and governing acceptable electronic mail. The Appalachian School of Law did not have such a policy. The Marshall University policy specifically cites electronic mail intended to harass an individual as a violation of school policy and states that the school reserves the right to take disciplinary action against anyone violating acceptable electronic mail policy.

Virginia Tech University has a policy of "Acceptable Use of Information Systems" that says that the school "considers any violation of acceptable use principles or guidelines to be a serious offense...." The school warns, "Offenders also may be prosecuted under laws including (but not limited to) the Privacy Protection Act of 1974, The Computer Fraud and Abuse Act of 1986, the Computer Virus Eradication Act of 1989, Interstate Transportation of Stolen Property, the Virginia Computer Crimes Act, and the Electronic Communications Privacy Act."

Virginia Tech put a bite into its policy in the mid-1990s. The school applied its "student life" policy prohibiting works or acts that constitute "abusive conduct," specifically conduct that demeans, intimidates, threatens, or otherwise interferes with another person's rights, actions, or comfort, to both off-line and online conduct. Indeed, the school's administration sanctioned a student for posting an anti-gay message on an internet site.

Hate mail has become a predominant issue for universities and colleges throughout the United States. Schools everywhere (but not the Appalachian School of Law) have reacted to the threat by implementing policies to curtail abusive online traffic. George Mason University in Northern Virginia has a policy that strictly prohibits students from using computers "to harass, threaten, or abuse others."

Kathleen Conn in chapter six of her book, *Bullying and Harassment: A Legal Guide for Educators*, asserts, "Many students erroneously believe that the anonymity of the internet protects them. In 2000, the Boston public school system ended free Hotmail and Yahoo email accounts for students after two boys at the Boston Arts Academy had sent threatening emails to a female classmate who refused to date them. The district subsequently installed email accounts that could be immediately traced back to the sender. That same year, a Florida teenager was sentenced to prison after he had sent an email message to a Columbine High School sophomore threatening to finish Columbine."

* * *

Angie's family had asked me to be the family spokesperson at the first anniversary of the shooting. The school decided to mark the anniversary with a service that included a short presentation by a representative of each of the victims' families. Angie's brother, Joe, who was on the school's committee arranging the memorial, asked me to speak for the Dales.

I asked Sue and Danny what they wanted me to say about their daughter. They responded, "It is up to you, you know what to say; we don't."

I have made my living writing--that is what I do. I have written for policymakers at all levels of the U.S. Government from working-level members of the community to the President. I love to write--but not this. Writing has always energized me, but the thought of spending a few minutes writing about Angie left me drained. Where do you begin? What can you say that can capture her essence and the loss we feel?

Remembering Angie One Year Later

The memorial took place in the school's large, main classroom designed to resemble a courtroom. The victims' families gathered in the student lounge nearby. The mood was somber. As we waited in the lounge for the ceremony to begin, I briefly encountered someone who seemed to say so much about Grundy and the law school.

I stood to the side of the room, not wanting to talk to anyone. Inside I was trembling and wanted to concentrate only on what I had to say and do. I noticed a woman "working" the crowd. Eventually, she approached me and introduced herself. I do not recall her name. All I remember is that she portrayed herself as a very important local figure.

I had spotted her moving from one person to another, looking around for the next handshake and moving on. Something about her struck me as inappropriate for the occasion.

It was my turn. As she approached, I could not help but notice a sickeningly sweet odor of decay. The smell that comes from mixing too much strong perfume with body odor—the same sweet-repulsive smell of decaying plants, something akin to the odor you get when you throw out a bouquet of dead flowers.

The woman recognized my name from the program and thanked me for participating in the ceremony.

When one is under stress the strangest things become significant. I had parked across the street on the other side of a stream that runs by the school. I was not sure I was parked legally. For lack of anything else to say, I asked her if it was okay to park there. I think subconsciously I wanted her to say, "No, you have to move your car." That way I could move the car and keep on going; run away from the terrible two-minute ordeal that lay ahead of me.

She responded that I should not worry; if I got a ticket, I could come to her, and she would "fix it." As she said, "fix it," she strained slightly and the volume of her voice increased…as if to underscore her importance.

Her words and her tone said everything. Fix it? Her whole demeanor changed. The subject now allowed her to display her importance and influence. She took on the role of the "grand dame." I felt a sickness in the pit of my stomach—I suddenly felt as if I were going to throw up. Her "I can fix it" attitude repulsed me. She could "fix" nothing! The time to fix it had long passed. Her words said one thing, but her body language and vocal inflection said another. For just a moment I felt I had a view inside the nasty, smoke-filled rooms that "fix" things in Grundy. Before I could say anything, she spotted her next victim and moved on. In silence I watched her walk away, but the smell lingered.

From the school's lounge, we went to the courtyard—at the precise time of the shootings, the town's church bells rang—the noise was faint, even muted. We then walked to the courtroom where the ceremony began.

I don't remember much of what was said. I was concerned about making it through my part of the ceremony without losing my composure. I had practiced, practiced, and practiced again. Janice and I had stayed at Angie's house the night before where I stood next to the kitchen counter to read and reread my two pages. The next morning, I rehearsed over and over again.

Would I say the right things? Would Angie's family find comfort in my words? Could I even make it through the dreaded two minutes?

Janice had encouraged me. "This is a big honor; they have chosen you to be the family's spokesman. If there is any doubt who speaks for the Dales, it will disappear today." When I wanted to stop, she insisted that I keep practicing. Each reading was an ordeal. It was difficult for me to read and for Janice to listen. Shortly after I started practicing, she went into the living room and sat where I wouldn't see her cry. Every time I read my words the hate, the anger, the anguish, and depression flooded in—my goal was to be robotic—to build some barrier between the words I was going to speak and the pain I felt inside.

I was the second family representative to speak. The committee had decided to go in alphabetical order of the victim's last names: Blackwell, Dales, Sutin. I really don't remember what the others said. I only remember following the program with my index finger as the ceremony moved closer to my name. When my turn came, I walked to the podium, my legs trembling:

Angela Denise Dales was proud of her heritage. She was the daughter of a coal miner and the daughter of a cook. Angela was a loving sister and devoted mother to her daughter, Rebecca. The first in her family to receive a college degree, she was the American dream—a small town girl on her way to making it big. A single mother who through hard work, intellect and determination was a success in everything she did. Angela was an honor student at Virginia Intermont College where she won the school's highest awards. She was proud of her association with the Appalachian School of Law, first as a recruiter and then as a student.

Indeed, Angie was at the top of her law school class and had been elected treasurer of Phi Alpha Delta.

How can we find the words to express our loss, the loss that all of us feel?

Everyone in this room who knew Angela feels the pain of her passing. There are no words that console Angela's family—there are no words in any religion, in any language, in any country that can capture the horror, grief, and anger felt by Angie's family one year ago today—and every day since then.

We have to move on—but how can we fully function questioning why she died? The family appreciates the students who were at Angela's side, but how do we deal with and fight the suffocation that wakes us in the middle of the night in a cold sweat—the suffocation of knowing that Angie did not get all the help she needed. Why did she need to die when the hospital was only six minutes away?

When Angela Denise Dales died, something good in every one of us died. Part of the soul of this town died. Part of the spirit of this law school died that can never be replaced. No tree, no flower, no plaque can replace what we have lost.

We will never forget you, Angie. We will always remember that you spoke words of truth, kindness and encouragement to family and friends alike. The family will try to live every day to the fullest we can as a tribute to you—the young woman who reveled in life and all that life offers. Your passing has made all of us remember that if we have something to say to a loved one, say it lovingly.

Say it as if we would never have another day with them—we must make every second of every day count.

We miss you every moment of every day Angie. We will never forget you. We will see that your daughter, Rebecca, grows up and has every opportunity to fulfill all the dreams you had for her. We will always love you.

Lucius Ellsworth

I had made it all the way to the last paragraph—composed. But when I said Rebecca's name I stopped. I started the sentence again; again I stopped. It took me four times to get Rebecca's name out without stopping; four times before I could finish.

As I walked back to my seat, no one looked me in the face. The only sound was that of muffled crying.

The next thing I remember is the President of the Law School, Lucius Ellsworth, coming up to Janice and me and shaking our hands. He was visibly shaken and seemed unnerved by the ceremony. He thanked me for my participation. I found out later from Joe Dales that Ellsworth had volunteered to him that the school had liability insurance.

In the courtroom lobby, the Dales family stood at the top of the steps on the right. Everyone filing out of the room made a wide path around us. Two students and two family friends joined us. No one else broke ranks with the school.

Wendy Davis

On the first anniversary of the shooting, Wendy Davis, Dean of Students and Assistant Professor at the Appalachian School of Law, wrote an article in the Stetson Law Review, Vol. XXXII pages 159-170. Ms. Davis' article was a flawed tribute to those who died and those who were wounded on January 16, 2002. Professor Davis' article contains some useful insights on dealing with significant tragedies, including a "Checklist for Actions After Crisis." The insights and list are worthwhile for all school administrators to read, but Professor Davis' writing is notable for one colossal absence. Nowhere does she say that if a school does not have security, the establishment of campus security should be the priority to prevent future tragedies. Nowhere does she even attempt to examine the factors that led to the shootings.

Professor Davis asserts that "support from the Grundy community, the community of law schools, and the students was wonderful." Yes, it was in many respects. But she goes on to qualify for some of the support. "The victims' families were invited to participate in all ceremonies and as many events as possible, including the graduation." The last item on the checklist reads: "Include the victims' families in ceremonies when appropriate." Who defines what is appropriate? Indeed, just what is appropriate? What is inappropriate?

If high-level politicians come to Grundy to honor the dead, it is inappropriate and insensitive to include the Blackwell and Sutin families but leave out the Dales. Yet this is what happened at the Appalachian School of Law. The message I heard Professor Davis and her colleagues at the law school say was, "There, there. We feel your pain, but you have to understand your place. We only want you here when appropriate, and we will determine what is appropriate and what is not."

The "Law of Consistency"

From far and near, celebrities made their pilgrimages to Grundy. There have been many photo ops—all minus the Dales. Senator Warner, former Attorney General Janet Reno, Ken Starr, and F. Lee Bailey came. All the VIPs were consistent in their expressions of support for the school and the rule of law. F. Lee Bailey, in his comments to the student body, said, "The god of common law is not justice. The god of common law is consistency." The Appalachian School of Law abides by this god—the school is consistent in ignoring the Dales family when any celebrities are involved. It would seem that the Appalachian School of Law feels that a retired coal miner and retired school cook are not appropriate at functions when the high rollers come to town.

Item 31 on Professor Davis' checklist reads: "Consider awarding posthumous degrees to deceased students." At first, the school considered doing so but then set aside any thought of such an honor, deciding that awarding said degrees was not appropriate.

It's true that the school did name the student administrative center after Angie, and the school did erect a plaque in her honor in the main lobby. The school did plant a tree for Angie next to the ones for Dean Sutin and Professor Blackwell, and the school does hold a run every year to benefit the victims and their families. However, the fact remains that the Dales' presence is not deemed appropriate in certain social settings.

The double-speak is heartbreaking, but it is everywhere. Officials refuse to answer basic questions. Everyone counsels the victims' families to move on. We can only move on when our questions are answered—in plain English. We have read answers to these questions in the press, but they are often inconsistent, or they contradict the facts as we understand them.

A Question of Accountability

About a year after Angie's death, as I continued to investigate the circumstances surrounding the murders, I realized I knew nothing about the court system in my home state. How does the judicial system work in Virginia? How have the courts reacted to acts of violence in schools or the workplace? I simply did not know. Now I do.

The Question of Guns

The power of the gun permeates all aspects of our society, and we wonder why Peter Odighizuwa turned a weapon on people he perceived had insulted him. No, the answer is not the loss of Christian values—the fact is that those values have been hijacked by members of the radical right—including some members of the clergy.

Stopping violence begins by protecting wives and children from husbands who batter, by keeping guns out of the hands of violent people. How can a country claim to be the greatest on earth, founded on Christian family values—yet have a domestic violence problem that has reached epidemic proportions? We can have laws that protect human life and still own guns. This is not an either/or situation. Unfortunately, powerful interest groups block any move to prevent the mentally unbalanced from buying guns.

As with so many problems, there is no simple answer. Somehow, private property, the right to bear arms, and Christianity have become intertwined—an unholy trinity of values.

Holding People Responsible

Off the record, one of the attorneys we talked to cited a case he had in the Norfolk/Virginia Beach area where the employee of a store severely beat and raped a customer. The store owner knew the employee had a history of violence and sexual battery, yet hired him. The jury ruled in favor of the woman, awarding her a sizable settlement. The defense attorneys threatened to appeal the case to the Virginia Supreme Court, where all parties knew the appeal would win. The court is reluctant to make any private business responsible for the actions of their employees—even if the employer has prior knowledge of the employee's violent tendencies. The result was an out-of-court settlement.

The same attorney went a step further. He said that in Virginia, whenever legislation is proposed that would hold employers—read private organizations such as the Appalachian School of Law—responsible for the actions of their employees, developers and builders use money, power, and influence to ensure that the proposal goes nowhere.

The Virginia Supreme Court, in contrast to the Supreme Courts of other states, consistently rules that private businesses, even with prior knowledge of criminal activity including violence, owe no duty to warn or protect anyone on its premises.

Michael Dudas vs. Glenwood Golf Club, Inc.

A case in point is that of Michael Dudas. On November 1, 1997, Michael Dudas, a business invitee, was playing golf at the 18-hole public golf course operated by Glenwood Golf Club, Inc. Court documents state that while playing near the 13th hole, Dudas and a companion were confronted by two men, trespassers, and robbed at gunpoint. One of the assailants shot Dudas in the leg.

Dudas filed for legal compensation, saying that in the month preceding this robbery there had been "at least two robberies of business invitees, one with gunfire, [at] the Glenwood Golf Club at the 7th and 13th holes. The assailants," the court papers continue, "had not been apprehended. The motion for judgment filed on Dudas' behalf contained three counts of negligence against Glenwood Golf Club.

The lower courts in Virginia sided with the Glenwood Golf Club, and Dudas took his case to the Virginia Supreme Court. The Supreme Court upheld the lower court, stating, "We have consistently adhered to the rule that the owner or occupier of land ordinarily is under no duty to protect its invitee from a third party's criminal act committed while the invitee is upon the premises. The fact that the prior criminal acts on the premises of Glenwood Golf Club were of the same nature as the criminal act that caused Dudas' injury does not change our analysis....."

The court's ruling also says, "Regardless of whether this previous criminal activity was sufficient to make the subsequent assault on the plaintiff reasonably foreseeable, we [have] narrowed the appropriate inquiry to whether this previous criminal activity was sufficient to 'lead a reasonable person... to conclude there was an imminent danger of criminal assault' to the plaintiff."

Thompson vs. Skate America, Inc.

The Virginia Supreme Court has narrowed its interpretation of responsibility in premises-liability cases so that very few plaintiffs can win their cases. I could find only one case in the recent past in which the court ruled with the plaintiff. Here, the court said in the case of Thompson vs. Skate America, Inc., "We have recognized that when a business investor has knowledge that a particular individual has a history of violent criminal behavior while on its premises, and thereby poses an imminent probability of harm to an invitee, the business investor has a duty of care to protect its other invitees from assault by that person."

In the Skate America case, Jonathan Thompson's mother filed a motion of judgment against Skate America, Travis Bateman, and Bonnie Mundie, Bateman's mother. The lawsuit filed by Jonathan Thompson's mother states "Without ...provocation, Bateman struck [Thompson] in the back of his skull, causing severe and permanent damage, extensive hospitalization and medical expense, and grave emotional damage." According to the legal action, Bateman had caused disturbances, arguments, and fights on several prior occasions. In fact, skating rink employees ejected Bateman from the skating premises and banned him from reentry on several occasions. He was under that ban on March 12, 1999. That day, Jonathan Thompson and Travis Bateman stood outside the rink, waiting for their parents to pick them up.

Skate America filed a demurrer that the trial court sustained. However, the Virginia Supreme Court held that "the allegations of motion for judgment were sufficient to state a cause of action against Skate America and, thus, we further hold that the trial court erred in sustaining Skate America's demurrer to the motion for judgment."

In other words, this is the one case where the Virginia Supreme Court held that a business could be responsible for injury to an individual by a third party. The whole issue rested on whether Skate America had a duty of care. "In Virginia, we adhere to the rule that the owner or occupier of land ordinarily is under no duty to protect an invitee from a third person's criminal act committed while the invitee is upon the premises." The Virginia courts also adhere to the principle that "before duty can arise with regard to the conduct of third persons, there must be a special relationship between the defendant and either the plaintiff or the third person."

Many people at The Appalachian School of Law, including the administrators, knew of Peter Odighizuwa's history of violence.

The more I looked into the circumstances around the shooting at the law school, the more I looked at the legal profession, and the more I looked at court decisions regarding individual rights versus business rights, the more intrigued I became.

In Virginia, judges are elected by the legislature. At present, the Virginia Supreme Court is made up of seven justices elected by a majority of both houses of the General Assembly. To be eligible for election, a candidate must be a resident of Virginia and must have been a member of the Virginia Bar Association for at least five years. If the General Assembly elects these justices, who elects the General Assembly? Well, large business contributions bankroll most politicians' campaigns. Newspaper editorials can make or break a candidate's chances of being elected to the General Assembly. The potential for conflict of interest is readily apparent.

Rockingham Publishing

In my research, I came across a ruling that was particularly disturbing. In May 1988, a thirteen-year-old boy and his parents agreed with the Rockingham Publishing Company that the boy would deliver the company's newspapers in Harrisonburg, Virginia. Due to the boy's age, under Virginia's child labor laws, Rockingham could permit the boy and other carriers of the same age to distribute its "newspapers on regularly established routes between the hours of four o'clock antemeridian (in the morning) and seven o'clock post meridian (in the evening), excluding the time public schools are actually in session." A year and a half after the then-thirteen-year-old boy took over the route, he was sexually assaulted one morning between six and six-thirty while delivering papers.

There had been three previous pre-dawn assaults of a sexual nature upon other young Rockingham carriers while they were delivering their newspapers. While two of the assaults happened more than two years before the one in this legal action, another one occurred only four months prior to the case in question. Furthermore, each of the earlier victims gave a similar description of the young man who assaulted them.

In legal terms, the issue was whether Rockingham Publishing had a special relationship with the plaintiff that would have required such a warning and whether the publishing company had enough prior evidence of sexual assaults that it owed a duty to warn A.H. (the paperboy) and his parents. The Virginia Supreme Court ruled that "Rockingham owed the same degree of care to A.H. that it would have owed if A.H. had been employed by Rockingham. And, given the fact that Rockingham assigned a fixed route and time for A.H. to distribute its newspapers, we conclude that the necessary special relationship existed between Rockingham and A.H. with regard to the conduct of third persons."

The Supreme Court then raised a technicality that puts so many Virginians in a losing position against private businesses. "Even though the necessary special relationship is established with regard to a defendant's potential duty to protect or warn a plaintiff against the criminal conduct of a third party, that duty, as in other cases of negligence, is not without limitations. A court must still determine whether the danger of a plaintiff's injury from such conduct was known to the defendant or was reasonably foreseeable."

Once you state that there are limitations, all you have to do to protect private businesses is set the bar so high that it allows you to reject evidence showing the attack was "reasonably foreseeable." Armed with this technicality, the court was then in a position to rule as follows: "Despite the special relationship, and even though the plaintiff's age may have imposed a greater degree of care upon Rockingham than it would have owed an adult in the plaintiff's circumstances, Rockingham had no duty to warn or protect him against harm unless the danger of an assault on the plaintiff was known or reasonably foreseeable to Rockingham. Since Rockingham did not know that the plaintiff was in danger of being assaulted on that particular paper route, we consider whether the evidence is sufficient to raise a jury question whether an assault on him was reasonably foreseeable."

The court, then, decided against the plaintiff's claim that his age and relationship to Rockingham created an additional duty of disclosure, "because the plaintiff has not met his threshold obligation of introducing evidence sufficient to create a jury issue on the question of whether the assault was reasonably foreseeable."

The plaintiff's charge that Rockingham gave "inadequate" and "deceptive" warnings regarding the risks of assault upon its young carriers during their early morning deliveries did not warrant a more complete warning. The court said that even if the publishing firm's safety literature, video, and safety whistles were inadequate, they "did not rise to a duty to give a more complete warning."

There is something wrong with the court's logic. If Rockingham did not feel it had a responsibility, then why did it spend time, money, and effort to have safety training for its paper carriers in the first place?

Then the court said that even if Rockingham's safety materials were deceptive (a matter they did not decide) the court "did not think that a duty was created in this case because neither the plaintiff nor his parents had seen or read any of the safety literature."

Two Virginia Supreme Court Justices—Justice Kinser and Justice Lacey—concurred in part with the majority ruling and dissented in part with the majority. The majority ruled that because the three previous attacks on paperboys had occurred in different locations, these attacks could not be presented as evidence. The dissenting judges eloquently argued the opposite. They determined that the random locations of the assaults make an attack on any given paper route more rather than less likely. In other words, if the prior assaults had occurred in only one area of the city or a particular route, then Rockingham would be justified in arguing that it could not have foreseen that A.H.'s route would have been the site of an assault. The dissenting judges also pointed out that "the fact that the assaults occurred in the same type of location, a paper route... [rendered] an attack on A.H.'s route foreseeable."

Other points raised in the dissenting opinion were the modus operandi of the prior assaults. This is a significant factor in whether or not the attack was foreseeable. "All prior attacks occurred in the pre-dawn hours while the three victims were delivering Rockingham's papers. The victims also gave strikingly similar descriptions of their assailants. All the descriptions included the same attributes as age, gender, race, and physique. In sum, the time and method of the attacks, the sexual nature of the assaults, and the similarity in the victims' descriptions of the assailant are fact sufficient to raise a jury question."

"Finally," the dissenting opinion said, "even though the first two assaults occurred four-and-a-half years before the attack on A.H., Rockingham knew that the assailant in the first encounters was never apprehended. Thus, when the third assault occurred four months before the assault on A.H., and the victim provided a description of the assailant remarkably similar to those given by the first two victims, it was then reasonably foreseeable that the danger to Rockingham's carriers still existed."

Dissenting Judge Kinser wrote, "For these reasons, I would reverse the trial court's judgment sustaining the motions to strike the evidence and remand the case for a new trial."

Editorial endorsements of papers such as those published by the Rockingham Publishing Company are keys to the election of the Virginia General Assembly, and the Assembly members elect the Supreme Court Judges. There is no evidence of impropriety in the case of A.H. vs. Rockingham Publishing Company, and I am not trying to accuse anyone of anything. But, the Supreme Court of Virginia would have served the state's citizens by bending over backward to ensure that a jury heard the case.

The Virginia Court System

How about the other courts in Virginia? The Court of Appeals includes eleven judges elected to eight-year terms by a majority of the General Assembly. There is a Circuit Court in each city and county in Virginia. The Circuit Court is the trial court with the broadest powers—it handles civil claims of more than $15,000. Circuit judges are elected by the General Assembly for eight year-terms. There is a General District Court in each city and county of Virginia as well. It is the court that most Virginians come in contact with because it handles most traffic violations. General District Courts' judges are elected by the General Assembly for six-year terms. Then there are the Juvenile and Domestic Relations Courts. These courts handle cases involving any person less than eighteen years of age. Once again, the General Assembly of Virginia elects these judges to six-year terms.

If a thirteen-year-old boy cannot get his case involving sexual molestation before a jury in Virginia, what chance does any of us have when confronting the power and money of private businesses? The molestation took place, no one denies that, but the courts don't want a jury to hear the evidence. Whatever happened to the concept that justice is blind? Justice is not blind to the interests of the powerful. The scales of justice tilt to the influential, to those with money.

"How could this happen in Grundy?" Why are we so surprised? Now, when the victim's family seeks explanations and answers—doors are closed at every turn.

After the shooting, Virginia's *Rural Electric Cooperative Magazine* ran a cover story on the revitalization of Grundy. When I read the article and saw there was no reference to the law school shootings, I was furious! The most defining event in that town's history is not mentioned. Instead, the magazine chose to run a rosy commentary on the rebuilding of the town's center.

How could you discuss the history of the town and not mention the shooting? The excuse is that Virginians want to move on—begin to move past the tragedy. But, ignoring that horrible event is not moving on. It is avoiding the underlying causes. Moving on is what everyone wants to do! Even the Commonwealth's Attorney in Grundy said the plea bargain with Peter Odighizuwa was best for the Commonwealth, best for all involved. That plea bargain allowed prosecutors to spare Odighizuwa's life. In return, he received six consecutive life terms plus twenty-eight years.

I cannot help but wonder how this settlement is best for anyone. Perhaps it is best in some eyes to move on and not delve too deeply into the events leading up to the shooting. Perhaps it is best to ignore harsh realities that would not be flattering to many prominent people and organizations. These realities would have surfaced in a court trial.

The Lawsuit

From the outset, people told us we needed to get an attorney. Even the Commonwealth's Attorney suggested we employ one. During the months following the shooting, as more and more of the facts began to emerge about Peter Odighizuwa, his violent behavior, the school's inaction, and the failure to get help for Angie, the more we realized we needed to hire an attorney. If we had any doubts about it, those doubts were removed by two things. First, the terrible meeting in the Commonwealth's Attorney's office on the first anniversary; second, the transcripts of the hearings held to determine Peter Odighizuwa's competency and ground rules for a capital murder trial.

Death Penalty off the Table

We showed the transcripts of the court hearings to a lawyer who said the prosecution's performance—as indicated by the documents—was among the worst he had ever seen. The transcripts indicated one of two things: either the Commonwealth's Attorney was in over her head and did not know how to prepare witnesses, or it was clear the prosecution was not going for the death penalty. Rather her goal was to strike a deal to avoid the trial despite her repeated assurances to the Dales that she would seek the death penalty.

We had to get to the bottom of the problem; we needed answers if we were ever to reach closure.

I began sounding out friends in the legal profession. Off the record, they said the evidence against the school was damning. Many just shook their heads in disbelief. But, they added, our chances of winning against a law school were next to zero.

Nevertheless, now more than ever before, I was convinced we needed legal advice. I was sure we had a case for premises liability or negligence. I knew we were not being told the truth. I also knew that finding an attorney to represent my granddaughter, Rebecca, would not be easy.

For me, the evidence was straightforward—Peter Odighizuwa had a history of violence; he was violent in both his personal and academic lives; the school knew of his violent behavior and ignored it. Angie bled to death because she didn't get immediate medical attention. What more do you need? I soon found out that, in Virginia, I would need a great deal more.

Fighting a law school would not be simple, particularly in a conservative state that–on the surface at least—preferred to emphasize the rights of corporations and businesses ahead of the rights of individuals. But it was clear, so very clear to me! The school had been negligent and ignored the signs of Odighizuwa's violent tendencies and acts. How could the facts be ignored?

The Bigger the Attorney, the Better

In the spring of 2002, I had begun to make inquiries about possible legal action. My thought was to get a high-profile, respected attorney to handle the case. If we had an uphill struggle--the bigger the named attorney, the better. My inquiries with local attorneys turned up several names of lawyers based in Norfolk and Richmond.

One local attorney recommended an attorney at one of Virginia's "finest law firms," a Richmond-based firm. He was a highly influential Virginian—a prominent member of the Republican Party who was plugged into all the right circles in Richmond.

A call to Richmond produced an immediate response. The attorney was not only anxious to take the case but went on at great length about his credentials and why he was the right man for us. He was, he explained, not a personal injury lawyer—but, he argued, that would work to our advantage.

Indeed, after the initial call, he was back on the phone with us within ten minutes, reiterating why he and his firm were the right ones to take the case.

I subsequently met with him near his summer home on Virginia's Northern Neck—not far from our house. Again, he put his best foot forward, mentioning his daughter and saying he would be crushed if this situation had happened to him.

What I was hearing sounded too good to be true. All the warnings about trying to sue a law school were simply not true. I could hardly contain my enthusiasm, telling my wife there was a chance! We would get our day in court!

I called the Dales with the good news and made arrangements for them to accompany us to Richmond so we could meet with the attorney. In my initial talks with the "prominent" attorney, he had indicated that we would have to put several thousand dollars upfront to offset expenses. That was no problem; Danny and Sue would bring the money.

What happened next was one of the most bizarre incidents of the whole process.

Meeting with the Attorney – High Hopes

The meeting was set for mid-April 2003. The Dales, including Angie's brother, Joe, drove up from Grundy the night before and stayed at the downtown Hyatt.

We met them there the next morning and joined them for breakfast.

From the hotel, it was a five-minute walk to the downtown skyscraper where the offices were located. There was an armed guard behind the reception desk in the highly polished lobby. We asked him for the law firm's floor and room number. He told us they had a large suite of offices on one of the top floors and pointed us to the correct bank of elevators.

The firm's reception area was comfortable, tastefully decorated in earth tones, with soft lighting that made for a welcoming environment. I checked in with the receptionist, but she had no record of our appointment. Somewhat flustered, she said she was sure it was a simple mistake and paged the attorney. He did not answer, and no one seemed to know where he was. I overheard someone question whether he was still in the building. The receptionist said she had seen him that morning and they would track him down.

The attorney's secretary finally located him and ushered us into a large mahogany conference room. I had a sinking feeling but just kept telling myself this was an honest mistake.

"I Cannot Represent You."

When the attorney appeared, he introduced himself, then got right down to business. "I cannot represent you," he said. "I cannot represent you because Dr. Briggs (the same Dr. Briggs who treated Peter Odighizuwa) was a consultant in a previous case involving my law firm."

I felt as if someone had hit me in the chest with a sledgehammer. I reminded him that we had specifically discussed that point in our meeting on the Northern Neck, and, at that time, he said the association with Dr. Briggs would not prevent him or his firm from engaging in a lawsuit against the school.

"I misspoke," he said. He then told us he would not try to sue the school. I was upset. I don't remember his exact comment, but his words and body language indicated he didn't think we had much of a case. What happened to all the hard sell; what happened to all the convincing that he and his firm were just what we needed?

I could not believe my ears! Where was the man who called my home pleading for us to give him the case?

Angie's brother, Joe, was visibly agitated. His face red, his voice trembling, Joe asked, "If this were your daughter would you be attempting to sue?"

"No," came the response.

I thought Joe Dales was going to come across the table and punch the attorney.

All I could think of was who has gotten to you? You son-of-a.... Someone has gotten to you!

We left the offices of this attorney—"one of the finest in Virginia"—in disbelief and stunned silence.

I turned to Danny and said, "I am so sorry, so very sorry to have put you through this. I don't know what to say. I thought I had it all worked out." I was still trying to come to terms with what I had heard.

As we entered the reception area, Janice was playing checkers with Rebecca. She could tell something was wrong by the expressions on our faces. "What happened? What's the matter?" she asked.

All I could say was, "You won't believe it." I just shook my head. I felt like crying; I had raised the Dales' hopes needlessly. It was as if my credibility had been raped.

Skepticism turns to Faith

Ironically, that experience tightened the bond between the Dales and Cariens families. Until that meeting, Joe Dales had seemed slightly skeptical of my motives. He may have thought I was using the tragedy for my own ends, or that I might be using the lawsuit to give business to a friend. From that moment on, he did not appear to question my motives.

We walked the few blocks back to the hotel, trying to explain to Janice what had taken place in the conference room. In disbelief, she kept asking us to repeat some of the details. Danny Dales reassured me that what had happened was not a problem.

We said goodbye in the parking lot and headed home—the Dales to Grundy and Janice and me to our home in Kilmarnock, an hour and a half away.

Disheartened, but more determined than ever, we pressed on.

Our search then turned to Plato Cacharis' office. I phoned his office explaining our plight to his receptionist and asking that their firm recommend a Virginia attorney. A few days later, Cacharis's receptionist phoned back and recommended another Richmond attorney. That lead resulted in another referral– to another of Virginia's "finest" law firms. This time I thought we had hit pay dirt.

My phone call to this attorney was met with the "sincerest" expression of sympathy from a man with the sincerest of soft Virginia accent, an accent that reassured and connected with the common man.

My hopes were high again—this time would be it. How could we miss? This time, we would not repeat our earlier mistake. Janice and I would hold a preliminary meeting with this attorney. Indeed before calling the Dales, Janice and I drove back to the state capital.

"My Sympathies Lie with the Law School."

At the appointed time, a heavy-set man approached us in the waiting room and introduced himself. His reassuring voice could not conceal the fact that something was amiss.

His appearance was disturbing. His shirt looked like he had slept in it, and bits of his lunch were spattered over his corpulent frame. Janice and I looked at each other as we followed him to his office.

The first forty-five minutes of our one-hour meeting were given to a narrative about how the attorney's sympathy lay with the law school. His words were a slap in the face. In fact, he said in a condescending tone, "I am going to write a check to the school."

The meeting continued to degenerate as the man's soft accent turned to patronizing sarcasm.

The attorney's mood switched back and forth from arrogance to disdain. Finally, he dropped the syrupy accent and asked, "What do you expect from the school? Do you expect them to have a guard at every door?" His tone now bordered on open hostility.

It was all I could do to hold my tongue.

I wanted to say, "As a matter of fact, if having a guard at all four entrances to the school's main building would have saved three lives, then yes, I do expect the school to have guards!" Instead, Janice and I remained silent. We knew that again we had failed to find someone to represent our granddaughter.

At this point, the attorney's rude behavior became apparent, even to him, and his tone switched back.

During the last fifteen minutes of the meeting, he did a 180-degree turn. Now, he was willing to entertain our case; perhaps we did have a point. He would raise the possibility of taking our case with members of his law firm.

Janice and I looked at each other, and, without saying a word, both knew that this was not the man for us; this was not the law firm to help us. We thanked him for his time and left.

Outside, in the parking lot, all I could utter was, "I cannot believe this. I cannot believe this."

During the ride back to Kilmarnock, Janice and I kept saying to each other, "Did I hear him right; did he really say this or that? Did he really say he was going to send a check to the law school because that was where his sympathies lie?" His words were not only insensitive but also absolutely incredible.

I was mentally and physically drained and exhausted. But, after about a week, I started the search again.

Carolyn McCarthy

I next contacted the office of New York congresswoman Carolyn McCarthy. Congresswoman McCarthy's husband had been gunned down in the Long Island train shootings several years earlier. Her office staff listened empathetically. Several days later, they called back to recommend that I contact Mr. Brian Siebel at the Brady Institute.

Mr. Siebel and the Brady Institute were helpful but indicated our type of lawsuit was not what they dealt with. They specialized in cases centering on the way guns are accessed—how the shooter acquired the gun. Mr. Siebel said that a person who is subject to a restraining order cannot buy or possess a gun. Unfortunately, this law does not apply here. Peter Odighizuwa's wife never got a restraining order. If she had, it would have been unlawful to sell him a gun. Later, Siebel expressed sympathy for our plight and recommended a Washington D.C. attorney, Pat Malone.

Again, we told our story. Mr. Malone listened but said he could not take the case. He referred me to Virginia attorney Ben Glass in Fairfax. Mr. Glass was interested in our case but said that in his opinion it should be pursued under the statutes pertaining to premises liability. Here, he recommended Peter Everett, one of Virginia's leading specialists in this field.

"Run the facts by Everett," he said. "If he thinks you have a case, I would be happy to work with him." Glass also indicated that if Everett were too busy to take the case he would.

"Do We Have a Case?"

On June 15, 2002, I emailed Mr. Everett's office outlining our case with the facts as I knew them. Nearly a month went by before he responded. Everett said that he had spoken with a law firm in Covington, but they were "skittish" because of "the distance." The Covington law firm indicated they would talk to a law firm in Grundy.

The result was that Mr. Everett found no law firm in or around Grundy to help him. Concerned, I asked him point-blank, "Do we have a case? If this were a member of your family would you proceed?" His response was that yes we did have a case, but it would be very difficult to win in court.

The Virginia legal system is "reluctant" to set a precedent that would make any private firm or enterprise responsible for an employee or anyone in a contractual relationship with them. Even if there is prior knowledge of the individual's violent behavior and the business or organization goes ahead and hires the individual, the courts are unwilling to hold private firms—including private law schools--accountable.

The picture beginning to emerge through the fog of legal jargon was that private organizations cannot be held accountable. If you are a private business in Virginia, you get a pass on responsibility. This concept in Virginia law of exempting private businesses from practically any amount of liability separates it from many other states.

No Recourse in Virginia

Had the school been a public institution, it would have been next to impossible for Angie's parents to sue. The laws of Virginia were written to exempt public institutions from premises liability lawsuits. So, it seemed that in a perverse way, we were lucky the Appalachian School of Law was private. If it were a state-affiliated institution we could not sue—even in the most egregious situations.

The more I thought about this, the more dismayed I became. If I understood the situation correctly, the interpretation of the law in Virginia indicates that even if a state school is negligent and your child is killed or injured, you have no recourse in the courts! I found a pattern of decisions handed down by the Virginia Supreme Court that granted blanket immunity to state schools and organizations—even in the face of blatant negligence on their part! I wonder how many parents know this when they send their children off to Virginia Tech, the University of Virginia, or any state school?

Through research, I learned that there are three levels of prior knowledge of violence under the law in Virginia. The first level is the violence that Peter Odighizuwa committed in his family life. This was well documented, but the law says the school could not be expected to know about it. Fair enough.

The second level of violence concerns his actions in the community. Again, there is documented evidence of violent behavior in the community—precisely when he threatened his wife in public and when he threatened co-workers while working part-time at a grocery store. The courts in Virginia have consistently ruled that a private organization or institution cannot be expected to be aware of this history. Well, maybe.

The third—and critical—level is violence on school grounds against other students, staff, and faculty. Here the evidence is clear; it is abundant. The school's administration knew!

Peter Odighizuwa's screams and verbal assaults against the faculty and staff cannot be denied. He was barred from some employees' offices because staff members feared for their safety.

History of Mental Instability

The unheeded indications of Odighizuwa's violence are mind-boggling. For example, the press carried an article by Chis Kahn quoting student Kenneth Brown as saying that Brown and his friends often joked that Odighizuwa was one of those guys who would finally crack and bring a gun to school. "He was kind of off-balance," Brown told the press. "When we met last year, he came up, shook my hand, and asked my name. Then, like five minutes later he came back and said, 'You know I'm not crazy, but people tick me off sometimes.' Out of the blue."

Shortly after the shooting, Ellen Qualls, a spokeswoman for Virginia Governor Mark Warner, told the press that Odighizuwa had a history of mental instability and that school officials knew about it! The governor is on the board of the Appalachian School of Law. If I understand Ms. Qualls correctly--even the governor of Virginia knew about Odighizuwa!

I would be hard-pressed to find better evidence of school administrators' prior knowledge of Odighizuwa's violence on the campus than the incidents just cited. This evidence clearly meets the threshold for justifying a jury trial.

Perhaps the most hurtful actions of a school official came in a classroom setting shortly after the Dales and three student survivors filed their lawsuit. In the presence of one of the students who lived after being shot, the professor mocked the lawsuit saying something to the effect that the plaintiffs only wanted money.

Perhaps the professor had forgotten that one of those survivors is walking around with a bullet in her and does not know if she will ever be able to function as a lawyer because of complications from that injury. Perhaps that professor has forgotten that a young child was left without her mother. To my knowledge, that professor has never even offered his condolences to the Dales family. Perhaps that professor has forgotten the ethics of his profession, ethics that would argue against such an unprofessional outburst in a classroom.

Richard Gershberg, esq.

Following the infamous meeting in the Commonwealth Attorney's office and our meetings with the other apathetic attorneys, I again turned my attention to finding an attorney. I told our son, now living in Baltimore, about our problems and my determination to get legal help. He said he had heard of a very good Maryland lawyer named Richard Gershberg. Perhaps he might be the person we were looking for, or he could steer us in the right direction. I phoned his office and made arrangements to travel to Baltimore on Monday, February 10, 2003.

Mr. Gershberg lived up to his advance billing. He listened politely as I went over our situation, the case as I knew it, and the problems we had encountered trying to find a lawyer in Virginia. He said premises liability was not his specialty, but he was willing to take the case. He then said, "Are you sure you want me? I have been told I have the look." For a moment, I was not sure what he meant. Then I realized it was the fact that he was Jewish.

My response was, "I am not looking for spiritual guidance; I am looking for a good lawyer." I should have added, "You appear to fill that requirement."

At last, it seemed we had found our attorney. Janice and I would not be parties to the suit. The suit would be filed on behalf of our granddaughter, Rebecca, by the trustees of Angie's estate, her parents. We subsequently made plans for me to drive Rick Gershberg to the Dales home outside Grundy. That trip took place in April 2003. There, the arrangement was sealed. All parties got along well. Rick Gershberg was honest and straightforward about our chances in what he said would be an uphill battle. But it was a battle we all wanted to wage.

Rick Gershberg joined forces with the attorneys for the three wounded students: Emmitt Yeary of Abingdon and Virginia and E. Brent Bryson of Las Vegas, Nevada. On January 15, 2004, they filed a $22.8 million civil lawsuit in the Wise County Circuit Court against The Appalachian School of Law, President Lucius Ellsworth, and Professor Dale Rubin.

Where are the Answers?
Where is the Justice?

For two years we waited. With no real answers forthcoming, my anger built. I am not wealthy, I am not clever, and I have no influence. I am no different from any man with flaws and strengths. How does an ordinary man fight back? The sense of hopelessness mixed with frustration was overpowering. Then I realized the one thing I could do was write; I am a professional writer. For thirty-one years I had made my living as a political analyst, writer, and writing instructor.

My answer has been to write articles and to write this book. But, the conservative press in Virginia has declined to print my words. I can write for all levels of the U.S. government—the NSC, members of congress, the cabinet, the President's Daily Brief—but my words apparently do not qualify for *The Richmond Times-Dispatch*, *The Roanoke Times*, or *The Fredericksburg Free Lance-Star*.

These same newspapers, however, gave extensive coverage to Odighizuwa's words–ramblings from his jail cell. The words of the murderer made better copy than the words of the victim's family. Clearly, Peter Odighizuwa's tirades would sell more newspapers. A few smaller Virginia newspapers *did* print my words, and for the Dales and Cariens families, seeing our words and thoughts in print helped us come to terms with our grief and frustration. We began to think that perhaps our words could bring about legal reforms to help prevent future violence on school grounds, but we did not have a 9/11 Commission to listen to us. The second anniversary was approaching and the pressure in me was building to say something; to do something!

Why I Decided to Write this Book

When I raised the idea of writing a book about the murders, my wife, Janice, strongly objected. She repeatedly told me not to write anything. "These people carry guns; you travel; I am here all the time. I don't want to be watching television and have a bullet come through the window!"

I wanted to say she was exaggerating, but I could not. She reminded me of the hostility we had encountered from our neighbors because our ideas on politics and religion differ from theirs. These are Christians who shudder at any four-letter word but get falling-down drunk. They are people of faith who refer to the Black workmen as "monkeys." Janice reminded me of these facts. "This is the climate we live in," she said. "Have you forgotten that if you even hint that you disagree with these people, they become irrational?"

There was no convincing her. In the wake of Angie's murder, how could I argue that my neighbor would not reach into his gun vault in a fit of rage and kill me, my wife, or a member of my family? I could not. I had no argument. I remained silent as if to acquiesce, but inside I knew I had to say something—for me, for the Dales, for Angie, for Rebecca—for all of us.

In January 2004, Janice spent nearly two weeks in Upstate New York helping her brother settle into his new home. This was my chance. The house was quiet with just the dog and me.

In the months before Christmas, I had thought a great deal about what to say. Indeed, Angie's murder was rarely far from my thoughts. I wanted to write an article. My work took me back and forth to Northern Virginia frequently. I used that time to listen to my favorite CDs and formulate my thoughts.

By the time Janice left, I was ready to write. In one four-hour period, the article poured out of me. By the time I was finished I was weak. Two years after the attack, it all came back: the anguish, the pain, the horror. Tears streamed down my face as I realized nothing was better. Two years later, it hurt just as much! The article I wrote appeared in two Virginia newspapers—but not *The Richmond Times-Dispatch*, *The Roanoke Times*, or *The Fredericksburg Free Lance-Star*:

Searching for Answers; Searching for Justice

Everyone sympathizes with the families when innocent men, women, and children are gunned down in the all-to-frequent acts of violence in this country. Who didn't agonize for the families and victims of Columbine?

Every parent feels a deep sickness in the pit of the stomach when there is a school shooting—a sickness mixed with relief that, thank God, my child was not killed.

Then, one day it is your child or another member of your family.

Two years ago a disgruntled student shot and killed Angie Dales, the mother of our granddaughter, and two faculty members at the Appalachian School of Law in Grundy, Virginia. Long years of pain and tears followed. I have watched Angie's father die from the anguish and stress; I have watched the grief on Angie's mother's face deepen as she copes with the tragedy; I have watched our granddaughter go—in a split second—from an exuberant seven-year-old to a morose child. The journey since January 16, 2002 has been terrible.

Time does not heal. Time allows you to come to terms with what has happened, but some wounds never heal. How do you "heal" the hours of screams from a seven-year-old when she is told her mother has been gunned down?

Time helps you live with the anger and rage stemming from the fact that a human being bled to death because she did not get help—when the hospital was six minutes away. Time allows you to think about her plea not to let her die—without losing your mind.

Those of us who are left behind spend hours and days saying if only she hadn't been in the student lounge; if only she had not canceled her lunch with a friend.

But she was there.

Indications and Warnings

In the search for answers, we look for warnings and indications of violence. Could this shooting have been prevented? Yes! Were there warnings that should have alerted authorities to the potential for violence at the school? Yes!

The indicators were there. They were clear; there were many. The Appalachian School of Law had no campus security on January 16, 2002.

Peter Odighizuwa, the gunman, was a threat. He had argued and fought with students and staff alike. Indeed, he was such a threat to the staff, that one employee—fearing for her safety—had him banned from her office. Others expressed their alarm to school officials, yet nothing had been done. He had argued and fought with students and staff alike. Yet nothing was done. The school did nothing and ignored all the warnings of danger time and time again.

Mr. Odighizuwa was not the only threat on campus. A year before Angie's murder, she received the following email from a fellow student after her computer accidentally sent a virus to another student's computer:

> *You fucking cocksucker. If you ever try to send me another virus again, I will track you down, cut your nipples off, and stick jumper cables in you and connect them to my truck. I'm not bullshitin'. Maybe the sheriff will find you hanging from a tree in Longbottom.*

Angie reported the email message to school authorities and the police, but the investigation turned up "nothing." No realistic investigation was conducted, and still, there was no campus security. The family's request to see the police investigation of the email has been denied. We have been told it is "confidential." Even the State Police's promise to retrieve the report from Richmond and answer our questions has never been met—after months of waiting.

Indeed, a State Highway patrolman has angrily lectured us. He told the family we should be content that Mr. Odighizuwa will get his punishment in the hereafter. We should be content with that! The police claim they do not know who wrote the email and that there is no connection to the murders.

How would they know there is no connection if they do not know who wrote the email?

In any case, there *was* a connection because this incident posed one more warning of danger to students that the law school knew about but took no precautions for the safety of their students.

Where was Security?

Our two-year journey has taken us to schools throughout Virginia. Is it unreasonable for us—or any parent—to ask that a school have campus security? No. Between thirty and forty Virginia colleges and universities contacted—all sizes, both private and public—have campus security predating September 11th. The Appalachian School of Law had none.

We have been cautioned not to ask our questions, not to press for answers. Privately, friends in the legal profession told us we would only bring more grief on ourselves. These friends even warned us that life would become difficult for us in the Old Dominion. Virginia's politicians and legal professionals will close ranks to protect the law school, they said. We have been warned that the legal establishment in Grundy has so many ties to the school and has so much invested in it that a retired coal miner and his wife, a retired school cook, will never get their day in court. From Richmond to Fairfax County, to Norfolk, to Grundy—the answers have been the same. Law firm after law firm has refused to take on the law school.

The American Bar Association says there is no more fitting response to the tragedy than to continue to build a program of legal education that promotes the rule of law, opportunity, and justice.

Where is Angie's opportunity? Where is our justice when those in charge do everything they can to keep the truth from coming out?

When the police and school officials failed to bring the author of the hideous email message to justice, Angie told her family, "I guess I don't amount to much." You are wrong Angie. You mean everything to us, and we will not let go of your memory; we will not let go of this fight for justice. On May 8th, Angie should have graduated from the Appalachian School of Law. Instead of attending the ceremony, we waited for answers.

Wherever you are, Angie, feel our anguish, feel our love. If you are calling our names, our hearts are answering.

Reactions and Warnings

I wanted my article to appear on the second anniversary of the shooting, but I waited on the advice of counsel. In the meantime, I gave a draft to the Dales for their approval. As the time for the graduation ceremony approached, the attorney gave me the green light.

After submitting the article to several large newspapers, I heard nothing. Next, I sent it to our local newspaper, *The Rappahannock Record*. The article appeared as a commentary in the editorial section on May 6, 2004. Later that month, *The Voice*, a biweekly paper near Grundy, printed it on the front page.

The reaction to my article was surprising and somewhat chilling. One neighbor called to say she had read it but would not let her husband read it because "he thinks he can fix everything. He cannot fix this, and it will throw him into depression." At the doctor's office, a nurse, giving my wife her allergy shot, closed the door and expressed her sympathy in quiet tones as if not to be overheard.

People in Kilmarnock with whom I had done business for years stopped looking me in the face. They talked about everything under the sun in painfully obvious ways to avoid discussing the shooting. The Black clerk at the local dry cleaner—the gregarious young woman who had greeted me each time I entered the store—met me with grim and watery eyes. She would not look me in the eye. Her body language seemed to say, "I am so sorry a Black man did this."

I wanted to tell her that the color of the killer makes no difference. Monsters come in all shapes, sizes, and colors. Instead, I said nothing. There was just silence.

My wife was in New York with her brother when I received the phone call supporting and warning me. I decided to tell her piecemeal about the warning. Her words had been prophetic.

From Southwest Virginia, I received a call from a man wanting to organize a demonstration in front of the law school. He and his wife wanted me to know that my article had made "official Grundy and the law school look bad." I could be on a "hit list," they said. They went on to say, "Be careful when you visit your granddaughter. Stop at every stop sign, and obey all the traffic laws. People have a way of going to jail in Grundy and not coming out alive. We have abandoned mine shafts here, and bodies could disappear." This couple indicated that if law enforcement officials didn't like you, they would stop you and plant contraband or drugs in your car. "Look over your shoulder at all times."

It was hard for me to believe what I was hearing. It took a while for the words to sink in. They had warned me that because I was expressing myself—exercising freedom of speech—I was jeopardizing my safety and the safety of my family. I started reflecting on what had happened since the shootings. Had I been unfair? Had I been dishonest? Was I overreacting or being too emotional? The more I thought about the phone call, the more bewildered I became. Had the phone call been a dream? No, it was not. Suddenly, I felt like I was living in a Hollywood movie, like *The Pelican Brief*. It was not wrong to be asking questions. It was not wrong to press for answers that might help prevent another tragedy.

My words did not make the Grundy elite look bad; their actions, or inactions, did.

The school president's responses to calls for security, such as "you women and your hormones…nothing will happen…you will be okay," made school officials look bad—not my words.

The hateful harangue of a State Highway Patrolman to the man whose eight-year-old granddaughter has just lost her mother in the state's worst school shooting makes the police look bad—not my words.

The disingenuous expressions of sympathy and empty offers of help from the Commonwealth's Attorney make local officials look bad—not my words.

The condescending tone of a prominent Richmond attorney to a man and woman when the mother of their grandchild has been gunned down makes the legal profession look bad—not my words.

An attorney's callous comment to members of the victim's family that his sympathy lies with the law school, and he is sending them a check, makes the legal profession in Virginia look bad—not my words.

The off-the-record comments of many attorneys in Virginia that we would not get our day in court, that we would not get a fair trial; these words make the courts there look bad—not my words.

The fact that an innocent young woman bled to death when the hospital was five minutes away makes the school and rescue officials look bad–not my words.

The arrest of sixteen public and private officials on bribery and embezzlement charges makes Grundy look bad—not my words.

I have spent three-quarters of my life as a Virginia resident. I have always been proud to say I come from Thomas Jefferson's state. Jefferson, the father of the Bill of Rights, guaranteed everyone's freedom of speech, the right to life, liberty, and the pursuit of happiness—the right to life!

Virginia Today

That was Virginia then; this is Virginia now. Today, a grandfather cannot visit his granddaughter without being afraid of retaliation for what he has written. Today, a man can murder three people, wounding three others, and the state will spend a fortune to ensure that he is treated fairly. But, when the family of the student victim asks for a copy of the court transcripts, they are charged ten cents a page. There is something terribly, terribly wrong in Virginia.

I could not help but think that this country invaded Iraq to bring the Iraqi people freedom of speech, freedom of the press, and a multitude of freedoms we—as a nation—proclaim so loudly. Freedom of speech that some of us have difficulty finding in today's Virginia. Did we go to war to bring Virginia-style freedoms to Iraq? I hope not.

Gunfight at O.K. Corral

Within weeks of the warning, I was teaching a class at the FBI Academy in Quantico, Virginia. During that three-day course, my colleague ran an exercise entitled, "The Rate of Violent Acts Compared in States With and Without Weapons Laws." The class was divided into two groups. One was to argue that if states had laws allowing concealed weapons, there would be fewer murders and fewer rapes. The other half was to argue the opposite.

One of the groups used the shooting at the Appalachian School of Law as an example of the wisdom of carrying concealed guns. The student launched into an emotional argument about the liberal press not printing that two students ran to their cars to get guns and help subdue Peter Odighizuwa.

The issue was so simple for this young man. The world was either "black or white." To carry a gun or not to carry a gun—that is all that counts. Where were the guns when they were needed to prevent three people from being murdered? How did these students' guns prevent a young woman from walking around with a bullet in her body for the rest of her life? How did other students with guns stop Odighizuwa from owning a gun and murdering three people?

He seemed to have given no thought to the fact that perhaps there is something wrong in a society where a man can beat up his family and then go out and buy a gun. The fact that innocent people were murdered and a child has been left without a parent; these facts did not seem to enter into the young man's mental equation.

What about the psychological scars on a seven-year-old girl because her mother has been gunned down? None of these questions entered into his thinking. The young man seemed to say carry a gun, shoot first and ask questions later; that is the answer to all life's problems. As long as he could run his life as if he were preparing for the gunfight at the O.K. Corral—that is all that seemed to matter to him.

What about the events that lead up to gun violence? People who advocate that we all arm ourselves seem never to look at other issues of the problem. They don't consider the deep flaws in our society that make people so anxiety-prone that they cannot function without a weapon at their side.

Once the subject of the Appalachian School of Law was raised, I used the opportunity to bring up Angie's murder, the email, and the warnings of the FBI agent who was leading the training. Unlike the law school, the Virginia State Police and the Commonwealth's Attorney in Grundy, the FBI zeroed in on the anonymous email message.

The agent described the email as having the specific signature of someone who might be a serial killer. He was shocked that Virginia officials had not followed up on it. The agent spent several hours with me. He said he wanted to turn the email over to the unit that had handled "the silence of the lambs." He asserted, "This email needs to be looked at by a criminal psychologist—this email goes way beyond that of a momentarily angry response by a normal person. It could easily be the work of a psychopath."

When I told him that the State Police had never gotten the necessary court papers to go to the server and identify who sent the email—he shook his head in disbelief.

"I know all about southwestern Virginia," he said. He then asserted that corruption—both in the public and private sectors—is an ongoing problem there. "It is ironic," he mused, "that southwestern Virginians wrap themselves in a blanket of Christianity, patriotism, respect for the law, and self-righteousness. Yet, nearly all of them seem to hate the federal government. Their elected officials and businessmen bilk their fellow citizens out of every cent they can at every turn." On this latter point, the agent seemed to be referring to the recent "Coon Dog" scandal. The scandal centered on the arrest of sixteen of Grundy's leading citizens, including the former chairman of the county board of supervisors. They were charged with accepting bribes in connection with the awarding of $7.6 million of federally financed flood cleanup contracts. All the defendants, county officeholders, and contractors, as well as one FEMA employee, were involved in the awarding of contracts to help the town of Hurley rebuild after the 2002 deadly flood. The press quoted the federal prosecutor as describing the defendants' actions as a "feeding frenzy of bribes, kickbacks, and inflated contracts. The bribes added up to $545,000, including expensive coon dogs."

"So I have been told," I responded. "When you drive through the spectacular mountains of the region you can't help but think that never has so much natural beauty covered so much evil and corruption."

"A good way to put it," the agent said. "I am from that part of Virginia, I have been shot and nearly died in the line of duty for the FBI, but I don't tell anyone down there where I work—they would disown me!"

I could hardly believe what I was hearing. Here was a former Marine who had put his life on the line for this country, yet he has family and friends in southwestern Virginia—chest-beating patriots—whom he could not tell about his employment. He could not tell them that he works for the FBI.

When I mentioned the warning I had received, the agent told me to take it seriously. He said I should never travel in Buchanan County or the surrounding area without a cell phone and tape recorder. He followed this up by saying that if the police stopped me, I should hit the automatic dial on the phone and have it programmed to my lawyer and turn on the recorder immediately.

The FBI agent volunteered that he had relatives from the Grundy area, and he knew all too well that they have their own way of handling things. He then asked for the names of all the people I had been dealing with in connection with the shooting. I told him I was not overly concerned about my safety, but he again cautioned me. "These people operate by their own rules."

I promised to do that and have since sent him the list of names. I did use the occasion to say that the only one I considered a threat to me was Officer Parker—the man who was verbally threatening during a meeting in the Commonwealth Attorney's office. I also relayed a mild concern over officer Santolla. "Why," I asked, "would he have told Angie's parents to make him look good if there was nothing wrong or he had nothing to hide?"

The agent agreed with me and said that is why he would like a list of all the officials I have dealt with. If something should happen to me, the FBI would have a place to start looking. He added that it would not hurt to have a life insurance policy.

Could This Tragedy have been Prevented?

C ould this tragedy have been prevented? The question would haunt all of us forever. What questions are fair to ask? When there are warnings of violence but no action follows, we have a right to ask, "Why?" When the death of innocent people occurs, family and friends who are left behind have the right to ask, "Why?"

Violence in the home, workplace, and schools should be of paramount concern to all of us. But, somehow, this concern gets lost in the aftermath of the emotions following a tragedy.

In the case of the Grundy shootings, individuals in positions of authority apparently never bothered to ask such questions. It never occurred to them to ask, "Could this have been prevented; how and what can we do to prevent further tragedies like the shooting at the law school?"

No one disputes that Peter Odighizuwa had a troubled existence. As we have seen, his time in Grundy was marked by repeated acts of violent behavior.

In our examination of the shooting, we have to consider whether it is unreasonable to ask why the school wasn't prepared for an emergency? My internet search based on the keywords, "schools, liability, security" turned up over 60,000 hits! Perhaps the most surprising discovery was the number of private security firms that specialize in school security—from grade school through university level.

Most Violence can be Prevented

The one theme that was consistent with all these security specialists is that most violence can be prevented if schools will heed the warning signs—"Readiness, Response, Recovery." The types of services these security firms offer include:

- Conducting school safety evaluations;
- Designing security programs to meet a school's needs;
- Formulating an operational emergency plan (including responses to intruders and weapons on campus);
- Providing on-site security training; and,
- Linking schools to private and public security organizations to ensure a given school has continuing access to the latest school security technologies and theories.

All of this information was readily available to the Appalachian School of Law long before Odighizuwa arrived on the scene. All of the information about these school security services was a click away on the computer. Administrators at The Appalachian School of Law apparently never raised a finger to the keyboard in the interest of security.

"Laying Down the Law"

"Laying Down the Law: A Review of Trends in Liability Lawsuits" is an article by Teresa Anderson, a senior editor at *Security Magazine*. It lists the most common areas for crimes to occur: parking lots, retail stores, exterior common areas, apartments, bars, and schools. Her study was based on 1,086 reported property liability crimes between 1992 and 2001—all predating the shooting at the Appalachian School of Law. Her study further showed that assault and battery made up forty-two percent of the crimes, rape and assault another twenty-six percent, and wrongful death accounted for fifteen percent of the crimes. Some eighty-three percent of liability crimes in the study were violent. Anderson's study indicates that schools are common areas for such crimes. Was the Appalachian School of Law not aware of these facts? If not, why not? The staff and faculty are highly educated and the very nature of their profession—the law—centers on crimes and bringing people to justice. Ms. Anderson's statistics only heightened our need to ask, "Why didn't the school have security?"

Another common theme throughout all the literature on school crime and security is prevention. Knowing the warning signs and acting to prevent crimes on school grounds is central to safety. For example, the literature from one private security firm, Atlas Security & Safety Design, Inc, heavily emphasizes that prevention best maintains school safety. The firm's expertise focuses on advance planning—the Appalachian School of Law had no such plan. In a section called "People and Security," Atlas Security & Design poses the following questions:

- Do guards patrol the grounds or challenge strangers? (The Appalachian School of Law had no security guards.)
- Do you [the school] have a good working relationship with the local police? (Apparently, the school did and does have "a good working relationship" with local law enforcement, yet the scene following the shooting was pandemonium.)
- Does someone in your organization keep up with advanced-security technology and the latest security-related ideas about building design?

(Had security been built into the school's design, Peter Odighizuwa might never have made it onto campus in the first place, much less from the second floor to the first to kill Angie.)

- Are all employees screened, and do you perform background checks before hiring? (How about background checks to see if your students have a record of violence and have threatened bodily harm to their spouses?)
- Do you have a clear statement for your security mission, job descriptions, and essential functions?
- Do you review, update, and document your security policies and procedures? (You cannot update policies and procedures that don't exist.)
- Do employees receive a copy of security policies and procedures, and do they sign that they have read and received them? (Again, there was no policy.)

Virginia: the Law Protects Businesses, not People

In Virginia, if the law is not specifically written to protect public institutions and organizations such as schools and universities from legal action, the law is consistently interpreted that way. The Virginia Supreme Court has said, "In Virginia, we adhere to the rule that the owner or occupier of land ordinarily is under no duty to protect an invitee from a third person's criminal act committed while the invitee is upon the premises. We also have stressed that before any duty can arise with regard to the conduct of third persons, there must be a special relationship between the defendant and either the plaintiff or the third person.[1]"

There is ample evidence that Peter Odighizuwa had a "special relationship" with the Appalachian School of Law. Ironically, one of the victims—Dean Sutin—had done a great deal to help Odighizuwa. For example, Sutin raised enough money to buy Odighizuwa a car, clothes, and food. I can find no examples of this being done for any other student. As already noted in this book, Dean Sutin helped Odighizuwa get a loan of $19,000 to reenter the school in the fall of 2001. There is evidence that the Appalachian School of Law bent over backward to ensure that Odighizuwa could continue his studies. For example, while other students flunked out, Mr. Odighizuwa was allowed to drop some classes so that he could remain a student in good standing and the school would fulfill its minority quota.

Since the lawsuit filed on behalf of our granddaughter was settled out of court, we will never know if the courts would have recognized the "special relationship" between Peter Odighizuwa and the Appalachian School of Law.

The fact that a settlement was reached certainly indicates that the administrators recognized that evidence of this relationship existed. They did not settle for the full amount of their liability insurance policy out of the goodness of their hearts. They did not settle because they had $1 million lying around and didn't know what to do with it. The administration settled because it was concerned that even in Virginia it would be found culpable.

In settling the lawsuit to avoid going to trial, the school said it did nothing wrong; it admitted no guilt. If true, then in Virginia—the way the law is interpreted—the school could easily have won because even when a "special relationship" exists, and the Virginia Supreme Court acknowledges that it exists, the court would rule that the business owner has no obligation to protect anyone.

In the 1987 case of Wright v. Webb[2] the court addressed the "special relationship" between a business owner and invitee. The court held that "despite the existence of that special relationship, the business owner does not owe a duty of care to protect its invitee unless it knows that criminal assaults against persons are occurring, or are about to occur on the premises which indicate an imminent probability of harm to [its] invitee." The court went on to say, "We further held that for the duty to be imposed there must be notice of a specific danger just prior to the assault." In our case, there was a history of Peter Odighizuwa's violence and threats on the school grounds. The Virginia Supreme Court, in other words, acknowledges owners have responsibilities in certain cases to guard or warn against violence. But the court itself in the case of Michael R. Dudas vs. Glenwood Golf Club, Inc.[3] describes this responsibility as a "narrow exception." The court sets the bar so high that private businesses are all but immune from prosecution. The Virginia Supreme Court says that in its view "to require a business owner who, through no fault of his own, has been victimized by assaultive criminals coming onto its property, to thereafter give warnings of the remote but potential danger of injury from the acts of such criminals would unfairly burden that business owner in light of the potential harm such warnings could do its reputation and the loss of its trade which would inevitably result."

It is next to impossible to read the mountains of court findings and not come to the conclusion that the legal profession and judicial system in Virginia are more concerned about protecting businesses and profits than protecting human life and safety. The court seems to be saying that to make a business— whether it is a convenience store or a private law school—responsible to warn its employees or customers about potential danger is "unfair." Unfair to whom? It is unfair to Angie that she lost her right to life, liberty, and the pursuit of happiness. It is unfair to our granddaughter that she lost a loving and caring mother.

If you listen to the media in Virginia, you come away with the perception that the state is overwhelmingly a "right to life" state. But when you examine the actions of the courts you realize that "right to life" is only for the unborn; "right to life" often does not extend to the living. This right does not extend to a young woman sitting in the student lounge at the Appalachian School of Law eating lunch. The "right to life" in Virginia appears to be narrowly defined to fit the rights of businesses. To quote William Bennett, "Where is the outrage?" Where is the anger over this hypocrisy?"

Throughout the United States, the law does acknowledge "norms" of behavior in many professions. In universities and colleges throughout the country, including in Virginia, the norm includes campus security. Industry and professional "norms" are often cited in lawsuits. It is ironic that a school that trains lawyers to examine "norms" and "standards" would disregard safety norms.

Campus security specialists say that part of their job is to identify students who have demonstrated abnormal behaviors and get them help before something happens. What an elementary concept! Yet this simple "norm" apparently escaped the attention of the law school faculty and administrative staff.

Appalachian School of Law—No Security

The Appalachian School of Law had no campus security at the time of the shooting. Since January 16, 2002, they have hired a night watchman. The shooting occurred during the day, not at night. Students I have talked to report that his main function appears to be to sleep on the job. Throughout Virginia, other small schools have security and crisis plans in place. Schools such as Lynchburg College and Randolph Macon College have plans to respond to a crisis. The Appalachian School had no such plan.

I checked over forty institutions of higher learning in Virginia—private and public—and found that all had campus security predating September 11th. Only the Appalachian School of Law had no campus security.

The Appalachian School of Law argued that, technically, under Virginia law, it had no responsibility to have campus security—but in the American legal system, "technically" is the refuge of scoundrels. Technically is what allows people with connections--the wealthy and influential--to ignore legal standards, common sense, the norm, and common decency.

As much as any Virginia institution, the school understands that there are standards to which members are expected to adhere. This rule certainly applied to campus security. Indeed, schools throughout Virginia not only employ security personnel, but many have emergency response teams and action plans; the Appalachian School of Law had none—nothing.

A lawyer-friend in Northern Virginia (and our own counsel) told us that in almost any other state our granddaughter's case would be incredibly strong—but not in Virginia. She shook her head in embarrassment, saying that in Virginia when a law is proposed that would make state or private institutions responsible for the violence on their grounds—when there is ample warning and it could be prevented—that law is voted down. The wealthy developers in Virginia open their pocketbooks and make generous donations to politicians. Judges are invited to exclusive golf outings—fighting for the protection of our children on school grounds becomes a "frivolous lawsuit."

The more I researched court decisions, trials, and media coverage of those legal proceedings, the more convinced I became that a disinformation campaign against the average citizen was underway. The sad truth is that most citizens are not well informed on the law and court decisions. What they know is filtered through the sensationalism of the press. A very potent and successful propaganda campaign has been pulled together to discredit personal injury cases. By selectively reporting on high-profile cases, those who want to absolve businesses of liability have been able to hoodwink the public into believing the reason insurance premiums are high is to offset the cost of settlements. They don't tell you about the huge bonuses and all-expenses-paid travel of insurance company officials. Nor do they mention the lavish gifts, donations, and hunting/golfing trips that politicians and judges receive. The public is not told of some of the questionable practices of insurance companies in order to ring every last dime out of their policyholders.

Questionable Practices

I am reminded of an acquaintance who was once employed by a leading health insurance company. Her supervisor instructed her to turn down a certain number of claims—even though the claims were legitimate. Her supervisor stated that only a small percentage of the policyholders would appeal or challenge the rejection. The company would then pay those who challenged, but the number who did not appeal was sufficient to ensure the company's profits. This unethical conduct should cause Americans to question how closely their insurance companies are tied to the draconian drive to inflate costs for profit.

Readers may remember the McDonalds incident when a spilled cup of coffee burned a woman. Like me, you may have thought the claim was ridiculous, according to the media's reporting of the "facts." However, you may not know that McDonalds restaurants boiled their coffee at scalding temperatures and that between 1982 and 1992 had received over 700 claims from people burned by their coffee. Some of these complaints involved third-degree burns. Despite the injuries and the complaints, McDonalds continued to prepare coffee at 180 to 190 degrees Fahrenheit to maintain maximum taste. Other restaurants prepare their coffee at substantially lower temperatures—135 to 140 degrees Fahrenheit.

How many people know that the victim, Stella Liebeck, suffered third-degree burns over six percent of her body—including her inner thighs, perineum, buttocks, genital and groin areas. She underwent skin grafting during her eight days in the hospital. How many members of the public know the facts of any lawsuit? Our knowledge is filtered through interest groups with an agenda. We know what the press and the legal profession want us to know.

Many newspapers carried stories about the arrogance of McDonalds' lawyers, arguing that the fast-food chain serves $2.7 million in coffee every two days. The condescending and dismissive attitude of McDonalds' lawyers was not lost on the jury. Apparently, the jury decided that McDonalds' pompous lawyers dictated the settlement and awarded Ms. Liebeck $2.7 million in punitive damages—just the amount the chain makes on coffee in two days.

Lax on Workplace Violence

As a manager in the government, I was trained on my responsibilities—professional and legal. On sexual harassment perpetrated by one of my subordinates, I could be held responsible even if I did not know about it—because I "should have known about it." If the law takes this firm a stand on an off-color joke or remark that can be interpreted as "harassment," why is Virginia law so lax on workplace violence or murder? Not only should the law school officials have known about Odighizuwa's violent tendencies—they *did* know about them.

In Virginia, apparently, as long as you talk the good talk, as long as you spout the right moral words and family values, there is no need to take responsibility. There is no need to act. Look the other way, especially if guns, violence, or murder are involved! But, when it comes to off-color jokes or sexual harassment, you must act.

Few Answers, Little Justice

I cannot explain it; I will not try; I would like to believe it was Angie, but I cannot. During the week of November 7, 2004, for six days in a row, we repeatedly received the same two emails from Angela Dales. Each time the messages were identical. The first said, "Hello." The second said, "Thanks." Several times a day the messages would come in—always the same, first, "Hello" and then, "Thanks."

A Virus?

I told Janice it had to be a virus somewhere. Somehow a virus was still out there that had picked up messages from Angie's computer before her death. That had to be the explanation. Maybe it was the same virus that prompted the hideous email message that school authorities and the police were so cavalier in handling. Then, on November 12, the day the lawsuit was settled, the messages stopped. Could this be a coincidence? We want so much to believe it was Angie. We want to believe with every fiber that Angie was trying to talk to us, to tell us she was all right.

That was not the first unexplained event that occurred. Six months after Angie's murder, we returned to Cooperstown, New York, the site of our last vacation with Angie and Rebecca. It was a difficult trip; it was painful. The summer before had been perfect. We had been there on the Fourth of July, 2001. The weather was perfect; we relaxed; we had a great time. It was so good, so sweet.

Here we were again on the Fourth of July the following year. This time it was not good; it was not sweet; it was agony. Janice was having an especially difficult time—everywhere we went there were memories of the summer before. In the immediate aftermath of Angie's death, the stress had been so bad that Janice had lost large clumps of hair. The hair loss had finally stopped, but the stress was nearly as great that July in New York as it had been in the immediate aftermath of the shooting.

On our way back to Virginia, we were silent. Binghamton passed unnoticed. Scranton disappeared in a fog. We said little to each other. At Harrisburg, we stopped for the night. After checking into our hotel, we found a restaurant nearby. A very pretty young blonde waitress bearing a striking resemblance to Angie came up to our table, knelt, and said softly, "I'm Angela, and I will be with you tonight." She didn't say, "How may I help you?" or "I'm Angela, I will be your server tonight." She said, "I will be with you tonight." Suddenly tears flowed down my wife's cheeks. She felt calm; she felt warm; she felt life would be better; we knew we would recover. To this day, Janice believes the presence of that Angela was not a coincidence.

Even if the messages were from Angie, there was little solace for all of us on that bleak Friday in November when the case settled. The legal victory was hollow.

How much is your child worth?

What price would you put on the life of your child or the mother of your granddaughter? How could any parent decide what price to put on the life of his or her child? Is it $100,000 or $100 million—what sum of money will give you peace?

No amount of money can bring any parent to that point. That is exactly how Sue and Danny Dales felt when they left the lawyer's office in Abingdon having agreed to a final settlement on behalf of their daughter's estate and their granddaughter. The law asks you to put a price on the life of a member of your family, thinking that once you have settled on a dollar amount you will go away. The legal system wants you to stop asking questions.

For a set price, the lawsuit on behalf of Angela Dales' estate and the three wounded students agreed to a settlement on November 12, 2004. The final papers were signed on December 30, 2004. The school, its president, and Professor Rubin were off the hook for thirty pieces of silver. There were no winners. There were only losers. We lost someone we love, the legal system lost because no one will be held accountable, and every parent in Virginia lost because the state's schools have not learned what it takes to make our children safe.

Had the lawsuit gone forward, the school would have had to defend itself against serious accusations. Greater public awareness of the lack of school safety requirements might have led to an outcry for legislation to make our schools safer and keep guns out of the hands of mentally disturbed and potentially violent people. Such legislation would be a fitting tribute to those who lost their lives on January 16, 2002; a far better tribute than a plaque or tree.

Justice not Served

The suit may be settled, but justice has not been served. The sad truth is that the charges in the lawsuit—a toxic mix of incompetence, negligence, and bureaucratic bungling–will never be heard in a court of law. The unsettling and unexplainable behavior of school officials, law enforcement, and elected officials will never be held up to scrutiny. The result is that the conditions and factors making schools in Virginia unsafe will never reach the public. The mistakes committed by the Appalachian School of Law are doomed to be repeated, and other young people may lose their lives on Virginia school grounds. Many of these mistakes were repeated at Virginia Tech. It would be so much easier for us to find peace and move on if we knew the lessons had been heeded and the mistakes corrected.

Questions need to be answered. Police and rescue workers need to explain to our granddaughter why her mother was allowed to bleed to death for forty-five minutes after the shooter had been subdued. The hospital was less than five minutes away traveling at a speed of 30 mph. School, county, and police officials need to explain why there was no emergency evacuation plan.

The American Bar Association Looked the Other Way

We are waiting for a response to the charge that law school personnel "doctored" information to conceal facts from the American Bar Association; "doctoring" that allowed Peter Odighizuwa to return to campus.

Incredibly, the school's lawyers never denied any of these charges. The school's response was that the charges, no matter how true, did not warrant a jury trial. If the charge that a law school lied to the American Bar Association doesn't deserve being heard in a court of law, what on earth does? The falsification of facts, if true, is dishonest. Why the Appalachian School of Law would let these charges stand unanswered in public documents is a mystery to me. A denial of this specific charge, preferably a denial under oath, would help Angie's family move on and find peace.

The defense lawyers for the law school tried to insist on a confidentiality agreement that would prevent all parties from discussing the case. It appears that neither the school nor the insurance company wanted the information made public. Indeed, a confidentiality agreement was prepared.

But, when a lawsuit is tied to an estate settlement, and a minor is involved, all parts of the case must be made public. The judge would not allow the settlement to go forward unless all aspects of the case were made public.

Settlement Announced

On the day of the settlement, the Appalachian School of Law issued the following press release:

ASL Court Settlement Announced

Officials of the Appalachian School of Law (ASL) today announced that Hartford Insurance had settled all claims in the lawsuits filed in the aftermath of the tragic shootings at the ASL campus on January 16, 2002. The Honorable Nick Persin, Chairman of the Board of Trustees at ASL, stated, "We note that the full and complete settlement occurred within the limits of the $1,000,000 insurance coverage, that the Appalachian School of Law contributed $27,301.10 to the settlement, and that the defendants expressly deny any and all liability for those shootings."

Rebecca Claire Brown, Stacey Emilie Beans, Martha Madeline Short, and Sue and Danny Dales (co-administrators of the estate of Angela Denise Dales) earlier this year filed four lawsuits seeking more than $23,000,000 in the Wise County Circuit Court. The suits named as defendants, the Appalachian School of Law, President Lu Ellsworth, and Professor Dale Rubin. President Ellsworth commented, "This settlement permits all of the parties to this tragic episode to move ahead without protracted and expensive litigation."

The Appalachian School of Law welcomed the first students in August 1997 to the Grundy, Virginia Campus. The law school, which is provisionally approved by the American Bar Association, enrolls almost 360 full-time students this year and has 256 alumni in more than two dozen states.

For more information about the Appalachian School of Law, contact Lu Ellsworth, President, at (276) 935-4349 or see www.asl.edu.

December 30, 2004

Trying to put the best face on this public embarrassment, the school decided to emphasize that the suit was filed for $22 million and settled for $1 million. What the school failed to note was that the settlement amount was for the maximum amount of their liability insurance policy—there was no negotiating on that. The Appalachian School of Law was not rolling in cash. They did not have $1 million lying around and decided to settle a nuisance lawsuit.

It is particularly upsetting to read the school's comment on the settlement. The Appalachian School of Law's statement ends with a clear recruiting pitch—an attempt to profit from the tragedy.

The statement issued by the attorneys for the Dales was released on December 30, 2004:

Students' Case Against Appalachian School of Law Settles for One Million Dollars

Abingdon, Virginia attorney, Emmitt F. Yeary, who represents the plaintiffs, Rebecca Brown, Martha Short, Stacey Beans, and Sue and Danny Dales (co-administrators of the Estate of Angela Denise Dales), in their cases against the Appalachian School of Law, Lucius Ellsworth and Dale Rubin, announced that their cases had been settled today for $1,000,000. In announcing this settlement, Yeary said:

"These cases were settled today after a hearing before Judge Clifford R. Weckstein, Judge of the Circuit Court of the City of Roanoke, Virginia.

Judge Weckstein had been appointed to hear the cases because of the potential conflicts of local Wise County judges where the case was originally filed. The hearing was held before Judge Weckstein to approve the wrongful death portion of the settlement agreement."

In presenting the case before Judge Weckstein, Yeary had also stated another factor to be considered was how long cases would have taken to present in the courts of Virginia and also the possibility of the bankruptcy of the law school if a greater judgment was obtained against the Law School.

Although denied by the defendants the plaintiffs contended that the defendants were negligent in failing to properly warn the students of the dangers of Peter Odighizuwa who killed two faculty members and one student, Angela Dales, and wounded the other plaintiffs on January 16, 2002."

Yeary stated the fact the Law School was paying $1,000,000 certainly indicates that the Law School and the defendants took these claims seriously and were concerned and realized their potential liability and were not paying this amount out of the goodness of their hearts.

Yeary stated these young women, Rebecca Brown, Martha Short, Stacey Beans, and Sue and Danny Dales, the mother and father of Angela Dales, have decided to settle their cases against the Appalachian School of Law and the other defendants in the hopes of bringing some closure to the nightmares and sufferings they have been enduring since the massacres and shootings at the Law School on January 16, 2002.

The horrible events that occurred that day in Grundy, Virginia, were even more tragic because they could and should have been foreseeable and preventable if only simple precautions had been taken and the numerous warnings about the danger of the murderer had been heeded by those in charge of the Law School and had they not ignored those glaring warning signs time and time again.

Although the settlement of these cases today may in some small and pitiful way bring some closure for the victims and their families, the horror of the terrible day will never leave them. These young women and the family of Angela Dales, and especially Angela's ten-year-old daughter, Rebecca, will be forever scarred because of the senseless murders and shootings of January 16, 2002.

Unfortunately, no amount of money will ever take away their heartbreak, their headaches, and nightmares that will continue to haunt them and that they will have to endure and bear for the rest of their lives.

Nor will any money paid to them erase the scarlet stains of blood from the hands of all those who contributed to these terrible tragedies. Nor should the payment of any amount of money in any way ease the conscience of those whose actions and omissions contributed to the shootings of these young women. Nor should it in any way help excuse those who contributed to the death of Angela Dales, and who allowed her to lie on the cold floor at the Law School that day and bleed to death for 45 minutes after her murderer was apprehended.

Today, it is our hope and prayer that the bringing of this case and the suffering of all these victims, will not be in vain, but will be yet another wake-up call and warning to all the schools and others to whom we entrust the lives of our children with a reasonable expectation that they will take every precaution to ensure their safety. Those responsible for the safety and security of our children and our loved ones should never be allowed to blindly close their eyes and tolerate behavior that endangers others, especially where such indifference is a result of greed, naiveté, bigotry, or political correctness. They must be made aware that in America if they fail to provide appropriate protection and take proper precautions for our safety they will be held accountable to the full extent of the law no matter who they are or what they are or what their social position or status may be.

The plaintiffs were represented by Abingdon, Virginia attorney, Emmitt F. Yeary, Las Vegas, Nevada, attorney, E. Brent Bryson, and Maryland Attorney, Richard L. Gershberg.

Worse Lies Ahead

Unless the causes behind the events of January 16, 2002 are brought to light and corrected, the sad truth is that even worse school shootings may lie ahead. The Virginia Tech rampage is proof of that fact. As for the law school itself and the lessons it learned, their "heightened" security amounted to hiring a night watchman and issuing a proclamation that guns are not allowed on campus. In the wake of the seriousness of the shootings of January 16, 2002, the school's response has left Angie's family and me speechless. The shootings took place during the day. A night watchman is hired to protect against theft at night— not to protect the lives and safety of the students, staff, and faculty while they are on campus.

In response to the lawsuits filed against the Appalachian School of Law, its President Lucius Ellsworth, and Professor Dale Rubin, the defendants' lawyers filed a demurrer. Quoting from the defendants' own lawyers:

> A demurrer tests only the legal sufficiency of the claims stated in the pleading challenged. While a demurrer does not admit the correctness of a pending's conclusions of the law, it 'admits the truth of all material facts that are properly pleaded, facts which are implicitly alleged, and facts which may be fairly and justly inferred.' Thus, the sole question to be decided by the trial court is whether the facts thus pleaded, implied, and fairly and justly inferred are legally sufficient to state a cause of action against the defendant.

I was thunderstruck! None of the three defendants denied the truth of the charges made against them! None of them were denying that they knew Peter Odighizuwa had a history of violence. None denied they had heard staff and faculty call out for protection against him. In effect, none denied they had a role in this tragedy. Let me repeat what the demurrer says. It admits the truth of all material facts that are properly pleaded, facts that are implicitly alleged, and facts that may be fairly and justly believed. Do the defendants admit all the charges brought against them are true?

The defendants deny that these claims reach a level in Virginia law where they can be held accountable in a court of law. The Orwellian reasoning used by the defendants' attorneys defies description. What fact doesn't deserve the court's consideration or need to be heard by a jury? Time and time again, their words twist and turn into a convoluted distortion of truth, a distortion that is so very painful for the victims' families to read.

For example, one demurrer argues, "The allegations of Odighizuwa's verbal confrontations with law school students, faculty, and staff do not logically indicate an imminent probability of harm to the plaintiffs or that Ellsworth knew Odighizuwa was about to criminally assault anyone at the law school. The allegations about Odighizuwa's argument with Rubin shortly before the shootings do not logically indicate that Odighizuwa was about to pull out a pistol and shoot anyone."

How do the defendants' attorneys explain that Odighizuwa was banned from certain school offices because staff members feared for their safety? How do these attorneys explain female faculty members asking the school to hire security officers because they feared Peter Odighizuwa? How do the defendants' lawyers explain Professor Rubin's public statement that he thought Odighizuwa might punch or hit Sutin?

I believe almost everyone would describe punching or hitting someone as "violence." Indeed, the dictionary defines violence as "exertion of physical force so as to injure or abuse."

The defense argued that there was no allegation that President Ellsworth knew Odighizuwa possessed a gun or any other weapon. "Thus, the allegations do not establish that Ellsworth was conscious that injury probably would result from [Odighizuwa's] conduct..." The defense needs to be reminded that injury does not require a gun or any other weapon. President Ellsworth knew enough about Odighizuwa's violent behavior that he agreed to ban Odighizuwa from portions of the school grounds.

Odighizuwa's Rampage Foreseeable

The bottom line is that Odighizuwa's rampage was reasonably foreseeable. Indeed, Virginia law and the Restatement (Second of Torts) place the burden upon the law school to protect its students and employees from Odighizuwa de minimis. If Peter Odighizuwa had no business on school grounds on January 16, 2002, then he was a trespasser, and the school should have called law enforcement officers and had him removed from the premises. The law school's own manual makes it clear that it had—and has–responsibility to make the facility a safe and secure environment.

Despite the school's own high-sounding words, it did not have an emergency plan in place. A plan as simple as: "In the event of an emergency of any type, pull the fire alarm." Had someone, anyone, on the second floor pulled the fire alarm after Dean Sutin and Professor Blackwell were shot, the building would have been evacuated. The student lounge would have been emptied, and there is an excellent chance Angela Dales would be alive today. There is an excellent chance the three other students would have been spared serious injury and psychological damage.

The defendants consistently argued that they could not have reasonably foreseen or predicted Odighizuwa's actions. But time after time both Odighizuwa's actions and the school's reactions demonstrated that the shooting spree was foreseeable.

In a New York case[4], the New York Supreme Court criticized the lower court that focused solely upon the foreseeability of the exact manner in which a disturbance was precipitated at a concert that resulted in injuries. The New York court criticized the lower court for concluding as a matter of law that it was an unforeseeable intervening event that relieved the defendant of liability. The New York Supreme Court ruled to the contrary, that the fact that the defendant could not anticipate the precise manner of the accident or exact extent of injuries did not preclude liability as a matter of law where the general risk and character of injuries were foreseeable.

The New York Supreme Court said:

> *Here of course the general risk reasonably to be anticipated from dynamics of this large closely packed standing assemblage, was the outbreak of disorder or commotion necessarily precipitated or initiated by the acts of some third person which result in injury to some of those such as plaintiffs who were in attendance at the concert.*

The whole question of "foreseeability" is hard to pin down. Can anyone ever foresee the exact moment or cause that will trigger violence on the part of an individual? Of course not. When dealing with someone whom a doctor described as a "time bomb waiting to go off," how can anyone predict the time and place when the violence will take place? That is exactly the point. In dealing with an unstable person, the exact nature of the violent behavior or when or how it will occur cannot be predicted! But that he or she will be violent is predictable, and preventative measures can be taken. The law school's own actions indicate the truth of this point.

In the case of Turpin v. Granieri in 1999[5], the court addressed the concept of foreseeing violence:

> *Foreseeability is a flexible concept that varies with the circumstances of each case. Where the degree of result or harm is great, but preventing it not difficult, a relative low degree of foreseeability is required. Conversely, where higher degree of foreseeability may be required. Thus, foreseeability is not to be measured by just what is more probable than not, but also includes whatever result is likely enough in the setting of modern life that a reasonable prudent person would take such into account in guiding*

reasonable conduct…

We only engage in a balancing of the harm in those rare situations when we are called upon to extend a duty beyond the scope previously imposed or when a duty has not been previously recognized.

The Virginia Supreme Court time and time again, refuses to recognize the responsibility of a business proprietor to protect "its invitees from unreasonable risk of physical harm." The Supreme Court specifically rejected 314A of the Restatement (Second) of Torts. "Acts of assaultive criminal behavior cannot reasonably be foreseen.[6]"The Virginia Supreme Court reasons:

> *In ordinary circumstances, it would be difficult to anticipate when, where, and how a criminal might attack a business invitee. Experience demonstrates that the most effective deterrent to criminal acts of violence is the posting of a security force in the area of potential assaults. In most cases, that cost would be prohibitive. Where inviter and invitee are both innocent victims of assaultive criminals, it is unfair to place the burden on the inviter.*

The accumulative effect of Peter Odighizuwa's violent behavior clearly demonstrates that his shooting rampage could have been foreseen. Furthermore, if the cost of security is so "prohibitive" why do nearly all other institutions of higher learning in Virginia employ security guards? Why does every other Virginia college and university have an emergency contingency plan? The Virginia Supreme Court's reasoning simply does not stand up to close examination—at least when it comes to the shootings at the Appalachian School of Law.

American Bar Association Double Talk

If the legal system in Virginia leaves a great deal to be desired in protecting our children when they are at school, then certainly the American Bar Association should examine the allegations that the law school "doctored" its records in order to gain ABA accreditation. I posed this question to Emmit Yeary, one of the attorneys representing the Dales: "Common sense tells me that the ABA will want to look into the lawsuit's accusations of the school cooking the books. What will the ABA do?"

He responded, "Yes, common sense would tell you the American Bar Association should examine any charges that it is or has been lied to, but common sense and the law are often at odds. I doubt that anyone in the ABA will take note of, much less look into, the accusations."

"The ABA should be purer than Caesar's wife," I replied. "How can they turn a blind eye to court documents that charge a law school has not been truthful in an effort to pull the wool over the ABA's eyes?"

On February 7, 2005, I decided to test Yeary's assertion and sent an email inquiry to the ABA:

> *Does the American Bar Association have a board of review that looks into complaints centering on lawyers' or law schools' falsifying facts, figures, and statistics that might be presented to the American Bar Association for a school to gain accreditation? If so, I would like to file a formal complaint and mail you the documentation.*

Within an hour, I received the following reply from Kathryn Thompson, Research Law (ABA), Ethic Search:

> *Dear Mr. Cariens*
>
> *I am in receipt of your e-mail message dated 2/7/05. I am not aware of an ABA entity that accepts complaints against law schools based on representations made during the accreditation process. However, I suggest that you contact the ABA's Section of Legal Education and Admissions to the Bar directly to determine whether they can assist you. Their website is located here: http://www.abanet org/legaled/home.html*
>
> *The phone number is 312-988-6738 if you wish to speak with a staff person.*
>
> *In terms of complaints against individual lawyers, please understand that the American Bar Association is a voluntary organization; there is no requirement that lawyers be members of the ABA in order to practice law. The ABA is not a lawyer disciplinary agency and has no authority to investigate or act upon complaints filed against lawyers.*
>
> *If you wish to file a complaint, you may do so with the lawyer disciplinary agency in the state where the lawyer is licensed to practice. Bear in mind that the lawyer disciplinary agency will not be able to assist you with any underlying legal problems; their function is to make a determination as to whether the lawyer has violated any applicable ethics standards that have been adopted in your state. A directory of state lawyers' disciplinary agencies is available at our website at the following internet address: http://www.abanet.org/cpr/regulation/scpd/disciplinary.html*
>
> *To the extent that you have questions about what legal options there may be in this matter, I suggest that you consult with a local lawyer. If you are unable to locate a lawyer who can help you, you may wish to contact your state or local bar association's lawyer referral service. The*

ABA Standing Committee on Lawyer Referral and Information Service maintains a directory of lawyer referral services at the following internet address:
  http://www.abanet.org/legalservices/Iris/directory.html
  For further information on the law and how to go about finding a lawyer see the ABA Find Legal Help web page which is located here:
  http://www.abanet.org/legalservices/public.html

Kathryn Thompson
Research Lawyer, ETHICSearch

I found the email response disturbing, so on February 7, 2005, I phoned the telephone number she gave mend left a message asking to speak with someone about my complaint. I am still waiting for someone to return my phone call.

What should the average American think? We are taught that rule by law is the most virtuous form of rule. The United States invades countries to spread democracy and—incidentally—the rule of law. Over 3,000 young Americans gave their lives and more than 20,000 have been wounded in a cause that is now billed as an effort to spread democracy and rule by law. Is it unreasonable to ask that those who teach this law should be the most virtuous? Is it unreasonable to think that those who advocate going to war to spread this doctrine should be the staunchest observers of legal practices, rules, and procedures?

With one last try, I hoped someone at the American Bar Association was interested in the integrity of the schools that teach law. On February 28, 2005, I sent the following letter:

Michael S. Greco, President-elect
Robert J. Grey, Jr. President
American Bar Association
321 North Clark Street
Chicago, Il. 60610

Gentlemen:
On January 16, 2002, Dean Anthony Sutin, Professor Thomas Blackwell, and student Angela Dales were shot and killed at the Appalachian School of Law. Three other students, Rebecca Brown, Stacey Beans, and Madeline Short were seriously wounded.
The subsequent lawsuit filed against the Appalachian School of Law (now settled), contains documents alleging that the school doctored information pertaining to its minority enrollment. This "doctoring"

was done, according to the lawsuit, to distort information going to the American Bar Association, information that might have undercut the school's efforts to gain accreditation from the ABA. The suit also charged that the shooter, Peter Odighizuwa, a black man of Nigerian origin, was given preferential treatment as part of the school's efforts to have the correct minority statistics.

Counsel for the law school did not deny any of these charges. The school's defense was that they did not deny the validity of the lawsuit, they simply denied that the charges reached a level that warrants a trial. I would like to formally request that the ABA investigate the charges before granting the school full accreditation. If I were to lie or distort any information, any fact, or any statistic pertaining to any aspect of the law, I would be held accountable. It only makes sense that a law school should be held just as accountable as a private citizen for such actions.

David S. Cariens, Jr.

By April 15, 2005, I had received no acknowledgment of my letter from the American Bar Association. I understand they are busy people. I am, after all, only a retired civil servant. Nevertheless, I tried again:

Michael S. Greco, President-elect
Robert J. Grey, President
American Bar Association
321 North Clark Street
Chicago, Il. 60610

Gentlemen:
On March 5, 2005, I sent you a letter related to the murder of Angela Dales at the Appalachian School of Law. A copy of that letter is attached.
As of this date, I have not received a response from you. I would appreciate a response about the issues raised in the letter. Thanking you in advance—

David S. Cariens, Jr.

A nagging question arises from all our attempts to get at the truth. What happened leading up to that horrible day in January 2002? Even when there is credible documentation that a law school may have tried to deceive the American Bar Association—there is no one to complain to. There is no board of ethics! Where is the advocacy?

If I had covered up something in my past or distorted the truth to gain entrance to the Appalachian School of Law, I would have been expelled. Yet, when there is reason to believe that the law school may have done exactly the same thing—to gain accreditation from the American Bar Association—no one in authority wants to investigate. There is nowhere to go to investigate the possible wrongdoings of a law school.

I received no acknowledgment of either letter. I remained puzzled and upset over this silence. Then I found out that the new Dean at the Appalachian School of Law had served on the American Bar Association's accreditation committee. The fog in my mind began to clear.

Our legal system is based on advocacy—a system of supporting and defending. But at some point, there is a moral imperative that says when and what you are defending is immoral, corrupt, or dishonest. At that point, you should not protect it. You most certainly should not cover it up or hide it.

Advocacy is an essential element in our legal/political system. This advocacy is supposed to defend every citizen's right to be heard in court. But, when elected officials and members of the legal profession set the standards so high to protect one part of society—such as businesses—to the detriment of others— average citizens—then this advocacy system is badly flawed.

The silence only steeled my determination to find answers and expose the inequities of our system of justice.

Saying Goodbye

Saying goodbye is so very difficult. It is next to impossible to move beyond a tragedy such as the shootings of January 16, 2002. How can we say goodbye when everywhere we turn we see the same bureaucratic bungling and insensitivity in dealing with human lives? Yet saying goodbye is what we had to begin doing on the 19th of January 2002. On that terrible January day, the gray clouds were heavy over Southwest Virginia—almost as if we could reach out and touch them. It was as if heaven and earth were coming together to mourn. The mist mingled with the tears on our faces, tears that have yet to dry.

Angie's Funeral

The funeral home was overflowing, and not all the flowers could be brought in for the ceremony. Strains of "The Love Theme" from *Titanic* played in the background. That day, in that setting, we began bit by bit to rebuild. But it has been difficult to pull our lives back together because of the lack of sensitivity to the tragedy that appears to know no bounds. It is impossible to say goodbye and find peace when every day there are pictures of young American men and women who have died or been maimed in Iraq because of half-truths, bureaucratic mistakes, and incompetence on the part of elected and appointed officials.

Danny Dales told me it was particularly difficult for him to see those faces. He saw faces with the same dreams, promise, and gusto for life that Angie had. He thought of the parents who were in agony. A friend of his lost a son in Iraq. Danny told me—his face flushed and his eyes wet, "All I want is to be there to listen to the father's grief, to say I understand; your dreams, your hopes have died—there is an emptiness that nothing can fill. Much of what you live for has been taken away from you. I am here if you need me. I understand."

Everywhere we went, we found people with similar stories; stories of callous treatment and downright dishonesty when dealing with the victims of a tragedy.

Sue Fortuna

Some eight or nine months after Angie's murder, I was teaching a writing course in Northern Virginia. Sue Fortuna, who had been in one of my writing courses, stopped me in the hall during a break and asked if she could see me at lunch. This was not uncommon because students who have been in one of my earlier classes often bring me their work and ask for a quick edit before they hand it to their bosses.

Sue indicated she had heard of our loss and wanted to express her sympathy. Then she told me she had lost her only son, Brad, in a car accident on August 3, 1996. He was sixteen years old. During the years I had known Sue, I always felt a sense of sadness about her, but I never understood why, and I didn't think it was my place to ask. Now I knew.

Sue said that she and her husband regularly placed flowers along the road where the accident occurred, but someone had called the police to complain that the flowers were distracting; adding, according to the police, that the person who called said, "It is time for the family to move on." I could feel the anger start to grow in me.

An apologetic policeman told her that he had no choice but to ask that Sue and her husband stop putting the flowers along the side of the road. The Virginia Department of Highways removes flowers and memorials if they prove dangerous or someone complains.

The unfortunate truth is that just when you think you have seen the worst in human nature, you find there are people lower than you ever imagined—you hear about someone making this type of complaint to the Virginia Department of Highways.

Almost pleading, Sue said, "If only Brad had had a love child. Some part of him that we could see and touch would help." During the first year after his death, she waited, praying for some young woman to come forward with a child, but it never happened.

I could not help but think how lucky we were to have Rebecca. Rebecca allows us to move on with our lives. She gives us hope. For Angie's parents, Rebecca has been their reason for living. There are so many ways her mother lives through her.

Rebecca and Angie were inseparable; they looked a great deal alike, talked alike, and thought alike. If there is a God, then Rebecca is truly a gift from that God.

The Fortunas asked me if I would edit a letter they wrote to their local newspaper in Warrenton. The answer was "of course."

Memorial Justified

This letter is in remembrance of our son Brad Brooks, who lost his life on Route 211 six years ago. We have continually placed flowers on that spot since the accident, but a few weeks ago the Virginia Department of Transportation asked us to remove a wreath and refrain from putting flowers there in the future. Someone had complained that the wreaths were a distraction and that the practice had gone on long enough.

We find it difficult to believe that the flowers or wreath could distract or offend anyone. Perhaps the person who made the complaint has never lost a child or a loved one. The placing of flowers was our way of saying to our son, "We have not forgotten you and never will."

Time has helped heal our pain, but we miss Brad, our son. We can see his smile and feel his hugs in our memories. Every day we have had to deal with the terrible fact that he is gone. We pass by this spot going to and from work and the flowers and wreath help us feel closer to him.

We have always hoped that when someone sees flowers by the roadside for a remembrance of a loved one, they will take a minute to think about their driving and realize how quickly accidents happen.

Life is so precious and someone you love can be taken in just a few seconds. It is our hope and prayer that others who find solace through placing flowers at the site of their loss will not be asked to stop the practice.

Sue and Jeff Fortuna
Amissville, Virginia

The controversy in Virginia over whether the state should pay for and erect roadside memorials to those killed in traffic accidents opened a window on another part of the sorry state of affairs in the Old Dominion.

According to estimates by Virginia Department of Transportation officials, the program to erect roadside memorials would cost the state no more than $250,000. *The Washington Times* reported that one transportation board official, Harry T. Lester of Virginia Beach, said that $250 a memorial "sounds like a lot of money to me…. Why should we be doing this for free?" I sincerely hope Mr. Lester was misquoted or his comments taken out of context.

In February 2003, Virginia's Commonwealth Transportation Board voted to erect roadside markers in memory of those who died on the state's highways. The memorials will replace those placed along the road by the families and will remain standing for one year.

The press quoted C. Frank Gee, the Transportation Department's chief engineer of operations, saying, "We're not going to be judgmental…. We're trying to send a message about safe driving." In other words, the state will erect memorials in memory of the victims. At last, some sanity in government! At last, some recognition that those left behind are victims, victims with rights!

A Veteran's Widow

Another painful example of the shabby treatment of victims came to my attention while I was working at a major military base in the Midwest. A veteran of World War II, who had been held and tortured in a Japanese prisoner of war camp, died, leaving his wife bankrupt. His widow had been left destitute because the care given to him in the veteran's hospital was so poor that she had to remove him to a private facility. His condition improved, but the costs were so high that his widow lost everything when he died. She had to declare bankruptcy and, if it were not for her children, would be destitute. I could not help but wonder how many American families are in the same situation due to their injuries in Iraq. How many servicemen and women wounded in Iraq received inadequate treatment? How many gave their all for this country, yet their families have gone bankrupt and lost their homes?

The family wrote to sixteen members of the House of Representatives about their plight. Not one answered. The woman's son is in the military and is afraid to make much of a fuss or go public because he fears reprisal or retaliation. Now, let me get this straight. The U.S. went into Iraq to bring democracy and justice to a long-suffering people. We asked young men and women to risk their lives for this cause. Have they been treated the same way the government treated the wounded in earlier wars? Once the beat of the Iraq war drums died down, what did the injured have to look forward to? Inadequate care and families left penniless.

Deep Wounds

Everyone who knew and loved Angie is doomed to wander from now through eternity, asking, "Why?" We will never be able to recover from this tragedy fully. We will never get a satisfactory explanation or justification for this brutality. Each one of us will, at some point, in our own way, say our silent goodbye. Our lives are broken, and even if the pieces are put together again, the cracks will remain. One critical piece will be missing. The scars will never heal completely.

How can we say goodbye and move on when so many questions remain unanswered? We want to wash away what we feel so deeply: the hatred, the anger, and the pain. But hard as we try, we cannot. The wounds are too deep. We know one thing: we will not be torn apart by our rage, but neither will we go away silently. We will continue to seek answers. All we can say is, "Angie you have been taken from us, but we will not forget."

Misguided

Well-meaning, but misguided Christian friends bring their faith into conversations as if to nudge me closer to their belief, a belief that they mistakenly assume will help our family get over our anguish. One friend, in discussing the war on terrorism, suggested that God is punishing this country. She is sure, however, that he will step in at just the right time (implicitly when we have learned from our erring ways) to put this country on the right track. We will be saved, as a people and as a nation. God, she assures me, is all-knowing and all-loving, and there is a reason for everything. If God is so loving, so all-knowing, and has a reason for everything, then please tell me the reason Angie died. Once we know the reason, we will be able to start the healing. This is a straightforward request.

When I asked this friend, "Where was this all-knowing and all-loving God on January 16, 2002?" she answered in vague generalities. She reminded me of people who survive an accident where others die; the survivors often praise God, citing God as the reason for their good fortune. My question is: what was the reason for the bad fortune of those who died? If God so loved you that he saved you and not others, where is your Christian compassion for the families of those he did not save, those who are left behind?

Implicit in her words is that those who died deserved to die because they had done something wrong. They were being punished. Explain this to me—give me the specifics and the evidence behind your reasoning. Or was it that they were somehow less worthy? Again, tell me why and how. Had they done something wrong? If so, tell me what, so I can learn, grow, and understand. Had they done something to deserve their fate? If so tell me what. How did God make the decision of who would live and who would die? I'd really like to know how God applies these rules. I never get an adequate answer.

Other well-meaning, but misinformed friends tell us it is time to move on with our lives. That may be true and all of Angie's family and friends wish they could move on. But, far too many questions remain for us to begin a healing process. That is the simple, but difficult truth.

Another painfully superficial attempt at condolences is the phrase, "We know where she is." This incredibly cruel attempt to comfort is one of the most aggravating sentences spoken to someone who has lost a loved one. These words are usually said with a supercilious smile. In my opinion, they are not meant to comfort the victim's family. Rather, they are meant to comfort the person saying them.

I want to respond by saying, "If you know where she is then please tell me! I don't care how far; I'll go get her. Tell us where she is, and her father and I will go get her, so will her brother, and so will our son David. We miss her so much! We are all so upset; the pain has been unbearable; please tell us where she is and we'll go get her!" These comments allow the speaker to sleep; he or she doesn't have to examine what may have caused the murder. These comments allow individuals to avoid thinking, avoid the truth, and avoid coming to grips with reality. Such seemingly innocuous sentences are wrapped in self-delusion, allowing the person who utters them to wallow in self-righteousness. Once you begin to question the causes of a tragedy, you open Pandora's box—most people are not prepared to deal with these questions, much less the answers.

To those who rely on God's will for everything, to those who say everything is part of a grand plan, then where is the guilt? Where is the need for punishment? If everything is part of a grand plan, why not sit back and go along for the ride? Why do anything? Why bother with reason, thought, and logic?

The absurd extreme that follows from this line of reasoning is that no one is accountable for anything because it is all part of God's will. Okay, then let's start by doing away with the whole legal system. I'm confused by this preordination theology.

Another superficial attempt to console is the comment, "Let the healing begin." These four words are usually heard following some large-scale tragedy or killing: Columbine, Oklahoma City, or the World Trade Center. These words are often accompanied by another meaningless and thoughtless cliché: "closure." Those who utter such words have no idea what the words "closure" and "healing" really mean to the survivors. They don't realize that there can never be "closure" or "healing" in the strictest sense of the words. There are only brief periods of relative calm in our lives before the horrifying reality closes in again. Tragedies leave permanent scars. They may fade with time, but the wounds never "heal."

It is said that the line between humor and tragedy is thin; indeed, it is. The humorist George Carlin put it succinctly when he said, after one of these tragedies, we should say, "Let the scarring begin."

A truly thoughtful expression of compassion and condolence came from a student in a class I was teaching for the Massachusetts State Highway Patrol. What she said was kind and to the point: "I hope you find peace." Her words were so simple, so clear, and they helped.

Largesse of Stupidity, Incompetence, Lies, and Deceit

We will only find peace and truly begin to move on when our questions are answered. Only when the largesse of stupidity, incompetence, lies, and deceit is exposed will peace be remotely within our reach.

We will find peace when authorities in Virginia who have the answers find the courage to tell the truth; when they have the backbones to put their careers and pursuit of personal success aside and face the reality of what they have been sworn to defend and uphold—truth and justice.

Judge Moore, the judge in Peter Odighizuwa's case, early on granted a defense motion to bar Commonwealth witnesses from calling for the death penalty. The judge said, "[the] victims' opinion as to what the sentence should be is not relevant." The Commonwealth's Attorney did not object. If I understand the judge's words correctly, the family of Angela Denise Dales had no right to address the jury. Even Odighizuwa's defense attorney expressed surprise that no objection was raised.

The strange thing is that I don't remember any member of Angie's family abdicating the right to Sheila Tolliver or to Judge Moore to decide when and where we would voice our opinion about what penalty Odighizuwa would receive.

When the whole legal ordeal began, Angie's father said to Ms. Tolliver, "I hope when this is all over and I see you on the street, you will be able to look me in the eyes." After Peter Odighizuwa's trial was over Sheila Tolliver did not look Danny Dales in the eyes when they passed on the street.

How can we move on, how can we forgive when at least one professor at the Appalachian School of Law uses his bully pulpit to belittle the Dales family's efforts to seek justice in a court of law? He did this in front of a class that included one of the shooting victims; he ridiculed and belittled the victims' attempts to seek restitution and justice through the courts.

Moving on, so Difficult

Moving on sounds simple, but it is very difficult. No one has the right to tell the families of shooting victims how and when to move on. Until someone suffers the tragic shooting death of a child or other relative, that someone has no right to preach to the survivors about how to recover from the tragedy. This is especially true when those willing to give unsolicited counsel are not willing to tackle the legal and societal problems that played a role in the crime.

Every time we catch ourselves enjoying something or feeling good, we experience guilt—we feel ashamed for enjoying ourselves when someone who meant so much to us is not here to share that feeling. It is impossible to move on, when you pick up the morning paper and see the faces of young Americans killed because bureaucratic incompetence and lies sent them to their deaths in Iraq. And then you hear shallow and superficial phrases such as "A New Way Forward." What way forward do the dead soldiers and their families have? Each one of those faces brings the pain flooding back; we grieve again for them and for their families. We want to tell each and every one of the survivors—we understand.

In Virginia, changes may not come until every family has lost someone because of gun violence. The change probably will not happen until every Virginia family realizes the magnitude of the problem we face; the threat to our safety and the safety of our children. How many sprees of hideous crimes will it take before Virginians wake up to the need to keep guns away from individuals with documented histories of violence; out of the hands of the mentally ill?

How can anyone "move on" when the law allows a man to beat up his wife and then go out and buy a gun—even when a judge has ordered a "cooling off period." Where is the logic? Where is the justice? Where is the outrage?

Throwing Down the Gauntlet

This book is a call for help. It throws down the gauntlet to Virginians—particularly the men of Virginia. This book simply asks, "Where are your backbones? Where are your brains?" We can have our guns and still protect lives—the two are not mutually exclusive. Yet, many in this state ask Virginians to put aside their ability to reason and think and mindlessly follow their frantic call to eliminate all restrictions on gun ownership. They frighten hunters by saying that preventing the mentally disturbed, criminally violent, and spouse abusers from owning guns will infringe upon their right to hunt. Nothing could be further from the truth. They cite the second amendment, "the right to bear arms" while ignoring the first amendment, "the right to life, liberty, and the pursuit of happiness."

The Victims didn't Deserve what Happened

The victims at the Appalachian School of Law did nothing to deserve what happened to them. All three, Dean Sutin, Professor Blackwell, and Angela Dales were decent human beings whose lives were motivated by improving the lives of others. Their only "crime" was to be decent and caring—they paid for their "crime" with their lives.

Members of the legal profession pride themselves on the fact that "the law is blind." Sadly, the law *is* blind—it is blind to suffering, and it is blind to reforms that may save lives.

The law is blind to the victims of the January 16, 2002 shooting rampage. The victims are not just Angela Dales, Dean Sutin, and Professor Blackwell. Victimization extends far beyond the three wounded students: Rebecca Brown, Madeline Short, and Stacey Beans. The landscape of southwestern Virginia is littered with victims of that terrible shooting and the others that have followed.

Peter Odighizuwa's long-suffering wife and his four children are victims. They have lived with the terrible fact that their husband/father is a murderer.

Danny Near Death

Danny and Sue Dales are victims. For them, the consequences of the tragedy linger in ways both small and large. For example, on the morning of June 11, 2002, Danny Dales was home complaining of a severe headache. Sue knew something must be wrong because Danny rarely complained about anything. Sue wanted him to see a doctor, but he had a doctor's appointment that afternoon and said he would wait until then.

By late morning the pain was severe, Danny was nearly out of his head, he could not focus his eyes, and he was drifting in and out of consciousness. At times he was not sure where he was and didn't know his name. Sue called her son in Bluefield and within an hour he was there.

Joe found his father lying on his bed, dressed only in boxer shorts and oblivious to the world around him. Joe picked him up, carried him to his car, and drove him to the emergency room. The hospital did a spinal tap and diagnosed him with spinal meningitis. By then, Danny was utterly out of his head—delirious.

The next day he was evacuated to a hospital in Bristol, Virginia. Danny Dales' immune system was gone. The doctor in Bristol asked if Danny had been under stress. Severe stress depletes the body's immune system quickly.

Under Stress!

For the next few weeks, Danny Dales hovered between life and death. He did survive, but he was still suffering the harsh, lingering effects of his bout with meningitis nearly five years later. He could not sleep, his hearing was damaged, and the disease had weakened his thought processes and ability to reason.

The law is blind to human feelings. What was our relationship with Angie? She and our son never married, yet she bore our granddaughter. The lawyer who represented Angie's parents on behalf of Rebecca cautioned me not to refer to Angie as our daughter-in-law. He said that if there is a trial, the defense lawyers will use this point to attack us. But she *was* our daughter-in-law. That is exactly who Angie was; she became part of our family the moment Rebecca was born—and we will use any term, any word in the English language we choose to describe Angie's relationship to our family.

Who is any lawyer to define how I describe my granddaughter's mother? Where is it written in the legal code of the Commonwealth of Virginia that I do not have the right to describe our relationship with Angela Dales in terms that accurately fit the reality? Where is it written that members of a profession who rely on a form of English that is hundreds of years old have the right to dictate how anyone uses any English word to describe the mother of his grandchild?

Rebecca, the words in this book are primarily for you. You need to know how much we share your anguish, anger, loss, and pain. We make this promise to you: we will never stop seeking answers. We will never stop questioning until those who played a role in your mother's death are exposed and held accountable. We will never stop asking, "Why didn't you heed the warnings? Why did you let Angie bleed to death?"

Death does not frighten me, nor does the knowledge that all of us must die someday cause me alarm. Death is part of life. What frightens me is that a law school has not learned from the tragedy that occurred on its campus. The Appalachian School of Law blithely goes on as if it played no role in the tragedy as if it should not be held accountable.

Angie will not read the next great novel or see the new great painting, works of art that will be created in the period that would have constituted her normal life span. She won't see her daughter grow and develop. The loss is tragic beyond words. I grieve for her and what has been stolen from her. I grieve for us because of what we have lost. I am beside myself with grief because a person who was so in love with life has been denied her fair opportunity to revel in all that life offers.

The tragedy of January 16, 2002 is far greater than I had first imagined. The shootings on that day have made the Dales and Cariens families come face-to-face with the harsh reality of the superficial and manipulative society in which we live. Every day we are reminded that Americans in positions of authority, the people we put our trust in, will stoop to any level to protect their careers or feed their religious, political, or philosophical biases.

"I Can't Fix This."

Sue Dales closes her eyes at night, hoping against hope that she will see her daughter in her dreams—just one more time, she will hear Angie's voice. But try as she might, all she sees is blackness; there is only silence. Danny died a few years ago, but throughout his remaining years, whenever he held out his hand to touch his daughter, there was only coldness and tears running down his face. Rebecca Cariens waits for her mother's embrace, but there is only emptiness. The lights in our souls have been dimmed, but we will not let them go out.

Every man knows that when your first child is born, you experience exhilaration; you feel you can do anything and everything. Nothing is beyond you. If you are not invincible, this child has brought you close to that point; the child has shown you the true meaning of life. Then a senseless tragedy pulls everything out from under you—you come crashing down to earth and hurt in ways you never thought possible.

Danny Dales' words spoken on the day of Angie's funeral will always haunt me because I think his words capture what every father has felt at one time or another, "My whole life, I thought I could fix anything. No matter what was wrong or broken, I could fix it. Now I feel so helpless. There is nothing I can do. I can't fix this."

Possible, Probable, Certain

Paranoid, sick individuals seek revenge against society and those whom they believe have done them some wrong. It happened at the Appalachian School of Law, Virginia Tech, and in numerous shootings throughout the state. Virginia, in particular, seems to be fertile ground for mass shootings.

Thirty-two people were killed just six years after the law school rampage, and at least another seventeen were wounded on April 16, 2007, at Virginia Tech. On May 31, 2019, a mentally ill employee of the City of Virginia Beach went on a rampage, killing twelve and wounding four of his co-workers. Virginia now has the unique distinction of three of this nation's mass shootings occurring within its borders.

In 2019, more than 1,000 Virginians died from gun violence—an average of three Virginians a day. Homicides made up thirty-three percent of that total, while suicides accounted for sixty-five percent. These figures are from The Educational Fund to Stop Gun Violence (EFSGV), a non-profit organization affiliated with The Coalition to Stop Gun Violence.

Since the mass killing at Virginia Tech, approximately 142 people have been killed or wounded on school grounds in the U.S. These figures only scratch the surface of the total number of gun-related deaths in this country.

Americana

In 2015, nine people were gunned down at a prayer meeting in Charleston, South Carolina. In 2016, a mass shooting at an Orlando nightclub resulted in the deaths of forty-nine people and the wounding of fifty-nine others. The following year, sixty people were killed and 411 wounded at a concert in Las Vegas. Then, in 2018, eleven peaceful worshipers were gunned down at a synagogue in Pittsburgh, and seven others were wounded. And on, and on it goes.

Forty years ago, a mass shooting was a remote possibility. Now, mass shootings are viewed as a probable, if not inevitable, part of American life. The failure of people in positions of trust and authority to adopt measures ensuring public safety has resulted in more violent rampages.

Innocent people are gunned down daily, and often their murders do not even make the evening news crawl. We do nothing to keep guns out of the hands of people who are a threat to themselves and others: domestic and foreign terrorists, convicted felons, and spouse abusers.

Our legislators cut funds for mental health care despite the near-unanimous opinion by psychologists and psychiatrists that we could dramatically cut the number of gun-related deaths—and all crimes—if we put major effort and funding into mental health care. Instead, the conversation focuses on civil rights, specifically the Second Amendment and the unfettered right to bear arms.

The Founding Fathers

No one speaks about the civil rights of the murdered and maimed. Instead, the dialogue turns into a feeding frenzy of irrational, gun-toting emotions, hindering and not helping to tackle the root causes of gun violence.

If we want to play the "founding father's game," how about referencing the Declaration of Independence, which came before and paved the way for The Constitution? The Preamble to the Declaration of Independence reads: "We hold these truths to be self-evident, that all men are created equal, that they are endowed by their Creator with certain unalienable Rights, that among these are Life, Liberty and the pursuit of Happiness." Clearly, the founding fathers had the right to life as their first and foremost consideration.

We hear a lot about Second Amendment rights and individual freedoms, but what about the rights of murdered citizens? Granted, some do speak out about the rights of the injured and murdered, but those who do are often shouted down or threatened.

Our founding fathers wrote many documents contributing to our country's development. To concentrate only on a small part of one, excluding the other documents is intellectual dishonesty.

Where I live in rural Virginia, it is not uncommon to see a bumper sticker reading, "I Love the Constitution." I want to say, so do I. The difference is that I do not love one document to exclude the rest of the founding fathers' words.

How We are Viewed

When I travel and work overseas, foreigners frequently ask, "To feel safe in America, do you have to carry a gun everywhere?"

Is it any wonder I am asked that question?

Day after day, week after week, month after month, innocent people are mowed down in public venues. Places once considered safe have been turned into shooting galleries. Still, we do nothing to prevent the violence.

According to the Centers for Disease Control and Prevention (CDC) and The National Center for Health Statistics, more than 110 Americans are killed by guns, and another 200 are shot every day. The U.S. gun homicide rate is twenty-five times higher than other high-income countries. According to the CDC, firearms are the leading cause of death for American children and teens.

The Trace Organization[7] reports that as of December 27, 2021, there were 20,726 gun-related deaths in the U.S, excluding suicides. The same organization also reports there were 693 mass shooting incidents in the U.S. in 2021, an increase of 13.8 percent over 2020. As a nation, we are so immune to mass shootings that the vast majority of these rampages didn't even make the news.

Something is wrong with this country. Yet, we claim to be the greatest nation on earth.

Who Can We Trust?

I have taught Intelligence and Crime Analysis for more than thirty years and have always taught my students that our judges and justices, despite their personal leanings, would let the facts and evidence of each case guide their final decisions. Naively, I thought the courts and legal system were primarily free of political biases and prejudices.

I was wrong.

The Law School

As already noted in this book, an employee of the Appalachian School of Law told a student to destroy potential evidence; the school's president rejected female faculty members' requests for campus security; and a professor argued with the killer the morning of the shooting, failing to report the incident to school officials.

These were law school officials, men and women preparing people for the legal profession, and young professionals who were supposed to be learning the importance of the rule of law: truth, objectivity, and respect for the facts, no matter where the evidence leads.

How can we trust graduates of this—or any—law school?

Virginia Tech

In the case of Virginia Tech, school officials said they did not know the killer was violent, despite overwhelming evidence to the contrary.

Following the double homicide in West Ambler Johnston Hall at 7:15 a.m, the police found spent bullet shells at the crime scene but no gun. Investigators found bloody footprints leading from the murders to the ground level and bloody fingerprints on the exit door handle.

Two hours later, the gunman slaughtered thirty people in their classrooms in Norris Hall and wounded seventeen others. The killer prepared for the second massacre for nearly two-and-a-half hours after the first pair of murders, yet the school's administrators did not broadcast a single warning. Earlier, the administration had warned the campus about mold in classroom buildings and broadcasted a notice when a killer escaped from a Blacksburg jail. But this time, with a murderer in the middle of campus, school officials remained silent.

Later, Virginia Tech officials claimed they had no idea the student was violent, even though campus police had arrested him for stalking young women and sending them disturbing notes. During that arrest, the killer was examined by a school psychologist and deemed a threat to himself and others. Yet he was allowed back on campus without restrictions, mandatory mental health counseling, or supervision.

The killer's warning signs were so apparent that an English professor threatened to resign unless he was removed from her class. Several other professors complained about the soon-to-be mass murderer. And yet, the school claimed it was not aware of the threat the killer posed.

Virginia Supreme Court—Far Worse

The actions of a law school employee were terrible enough, but Virginia Tech officials ignored glaring warning signs, constituting gross negligence. Furthermore, the Virginia Supreme Court's allowance of a lie to be introduced into one of its decisions was tantamount to complicity after the fact.

The Pryde and Peterson families, parents of two students killed at Virginia Tech, refused to settle with the state. They filed a lawsuit, not for money but to get people testifying under oath and bring out the facts.

The trial was a devastating indictment of Virginia Tech. On March 14, 2012, a jury awarded each parent $1 million, adding up to $4 million. But because Virginia has sovereign immunity, the judge had to reduce the award to $100,000 each. The money was not the issue; it was never the issue. The two families wanted to uncover the truth and expose the school officials' incompetence.

Then Virginia Attorney General Ken Cuccinelli appealed the decision to the Virginia Supreme Court, one of the nation's most conservative state supreme courts. The court adhered to the political view that there are no situations where a person or organization can be held responsible for someone else's actions.

I foolishly believed the case against Tech was so overpowering that the Virginia Supreme Court could do nothing but uphold the jury verdict. But in what appears to be a politically motivated action, the Virginia Supreme Court overturned the jury verdict, removing all legal responsibilities from the state and university.

The court's unanimous yet error-ridden decision broke the law. Complete unanimity by State Supreme Court justices regarding an event of such magnitude is highly suspicious. Indeed, overturning the jury verdict may be evidence of just how far political bias—especially in the face of overwhelming evidence of gross negligence—dictates Virginia Supreme Court decisions.

It is against the law[8] for a Supreme Court justice to introduce false evidence into its decisions, but that is what Justice Cleo E. Powell apparently allowed to happen. On October 13, 2013, Justice Powell and all the court justices, in a unanimous decision, overturned the jury verdict.

Page two of Justice Powell's reversal contains a critical factual error. On the morning of April 16, 2007, Justice Powell wrote, "Although officers from the Virginia Tech Police Department were first on the scene, the Blacksburg Police Department led the investigation." In reality, the Virginia Tech Police Department under Chief Wendell Flinchum took charge. A legal agreement between Blacksburg and the university states that the police department (Virginia Tech) requesting assistance would retain control of the investigation.

Not every act of gun violence can indeed be prevented. However, many, if not most, of the shooting rampages I have examined took place because people ignored the warning signs, did not do their jobs, or lied. The tragedies could have been prevented. (For a detailed account and analysis of the Virginia Supreme Court's action in the Pryde and Peterson lawsuit, see *Virginia Tech: Make Sure It Doesn't Get Out*, High Tide Publications, 2015, pages 228-253.)

Afraid of Being Sued

Professor Helen de Haven at Atlanta's John Marshall Law School has written a great deal on gun violence. She was on the Appalachian School of Law staff when the mass shooting, as mentioned above, took place. Since that time, she has devoted much of her time and effort to examining problems with schools' responses to threats.

The most insensitive and depressing story is the one told by Professor Carol Parker and her colleagues at the University of Tennessee:

> *A law professor was being stalked and threatened with death by a student who was failing his class. He and his colleagues went to the*

administration. Sadly, he later reported, they simply stuck their heads in the sand and said nothing was happening. For the administration, this do-nothing strategy was a win-win situation. If they took action, they might get sued. However, on the small chance that the student carried out his threat to kill the professor, we figured that they would hire a cheaper faculty member." (Smith, Thomas & Parker: Violence on Campus Practical Recommendations for Legal Action.) Carol Parker's article is accessible free on the social research network (ssrn).

Things Have been Done and Can be Done.

Other nations have adopted effective measures to stop mass slaughter without turning into dictatorships. Their citizens' personal freedoms remain intact.

In 1996, following a shooting rampage that took thirty-five lives, Australia adopted the National Firearms Agreement. The agreement has ten regulatory reforms helping to protect average citizens as they go about their daily lives.

The last time I checked, Australia remains a parliamentary democracy, where people recognize that in the interests of the safety of society, all rights have limitations.

Despite all the talk about patriotism and freedoms, I assert that the U.S. does not protect its average citizens' right to life, liberty, and the pursuit of happiness. Protecting individual rights and curbing gun violence are not mutually exclusive. The following are basic principles I believe would dramatically curb gun violence and not infringe on citizens' rights as spelled out in the Constitution:

1. Adopt laws to keep guns out of the hands of those who are a threat to themselves and others;
2. Pass legislation to keep guns out of the hands of those who have committed violent crimes;
3. Support measures to ensure guns do not get into the hands of domestic and foreign terrorists; and
4. Ensure that guns are kept out of the hands of spouse abusers.

Finally, don't use the words: gun control. No one wants to "control" the guns of peaceful, law-abiding citizens. Those words play right into the propaganda of gun manufacturers and the National Rifle Association, whose goal is to make as much money as possible through gun sales—even if it means tens of thousands of innocent citizens are killed and injured every year.

Appendix

The Australian Regulatory Reforms

1. Ban on importation, ownership, sale, resale, transfer, possession, manufacture or use of all self-loading center rifles, all self-loading and pump-action shotguns, and all self-loading rimfire rifles (with some exceptions to primary producers and clay target shooters).
2. Compensatory buyback scheme through which firearms owners would be paid the market value for prohibited firearms handed in during a 12-month amnesty.
3. Registration of all firearms as part of an integrated shooter licensing scheme.
4. Shooter licensing based on the requirement to prove "genuine reason" for owning a firearm, including occupational use, demonstrated membership in an authorized target shooting club, or hunting (with proof of permission from a rural landowner).
5. Licensing scheme based on five categories of firearms, minimum age of 18 years, and criteria for a "fit and proper person."
6. New license applicant required to undertake accredited training course in firearms safety.
7. In addition to license to own a firearm, require a separate permit for each purchase of a firearm subject to a 28-day waiting period.
8. Uniform and strict firearm storage requirements.
9. Firearms sales to be conducted only through licensed firearm dealers and all records of sale to be provided to the police.
10. Sale of ammunition only for firearms for which purchaser is licensed and limitations on quantities purchased within a time period.

Endnotes

1   Gupton v. Quicke, 247 VA. 362, 363, 442 S.E.2d 658, 658 (1994).

2   Wright v Webb, 234 Va. at 533, 362, S.E.2d at 922, (1987)

3   Michael R. Dudas vs. Glenwood Golf Club, Inc., 261 Va. 133,540 S.E. 2d 129 Va. Lexis 5, (2001)

4   Rotz v. City of New York, 143 A.D. 2d 301, 532 N.Y.S. 2d 245 (1988)

5   Turpin v. Granieri 985 P. 2d 669 (Id. 1999)

6   Wright v. Webb 234 Va. At 531, 362 S.E.2d at 921 (1987)

7   The Trace Organization, founded in 2015, is a non-profit journalism outlet that is devoted to gun-related news in the U.S.

8   The Virginia Rules of Professional Conduct mandate that a "lawyer shall not knowingly . . . make a false statement of fact or law to a tribunal." Nor may a lawyer knowingly "fail to disclose to the tribunal controlling legal authority in the subject jurisdiction known to the lawyer to be adverse to the position of the client and not disclosed by opposing counsel." Rule 3.3(a)(1) & (3).

Acknowledgments

I want to thank many people—family and friends—for supporting the effort that went into writing this book. I must begin with special thanks to Sue and Danny Dales for their daughter, Angie, and her remarkable role in all our lives. Joe Dales and his wife Kay, I thank you for all the support you have given Angie's parents and our granddaughter, Rebecca—there are no words to express my gratitude.

I wish to thank my wife, Janice, who understood why I needed to write and find answers despite her reservations about my writing this book. To our oldest son David, this book is intended to tell you how much we all understand the depth of your pain. Our other two sons, Ben and Richard, and your families— you were there to support your brother through those dark days in January 2002. Thank you.

I thank Carolyn Miller and Maggie Strom—two wonderful editors of the first edition. You helped me take the rage and mold it into meaningful text. I will always be grateful.

Marty Petersen, a good friend, not only listened to me in those terrible days following the shooting but read the manuscript and helped me turn the book into what I hope is a compelling story. Thank you, Marty, for telling me not to let anyone remove the passion from my words.

Thank you, Richard Gershberg, Emmitt Yeary, and E. Brent Bryson, the attorneys who worked so hard to secure a future for our granddaughter, Rebecca Cariens—we are in your debt forever.

We thank all those who gave the Dales and Cariens families support from the bottom of our hearts.

This book was my first and is the book I consider my most important. A special thanks to High Tide's talented editor, Cindy Freeman, who read my words and suggested it was time to revise and update the book—and publish this revised edition. Thank you, Jeanne Johansen, owner of High Tide Publications, for agreeing with Cindy and encouraging me to launch this edition. Your support for all my writing has been invaluable. I am so fortunate and pleased to be one of your authors.

David Cariens
Palmyra, Virginia
May 2022

About the Author

David Cariens is a retired CIA officer —31-year career. Most of his time at the Agency was spent as a political analyst dealing with Eastern Europe. In this capacity he wrote for all levels of the U.S. government —from the President to the working level analysts and policymakers. Currently, Cariens is a member of the Governor's Commission to Investigate the May 31, 2019 Mass Shooting at Virginia Beach.

Cariens served in Eastern Europe and as an editor at the BBC-FBIS facility outside London. He headed the CIA University program teaching new analysts writing and briefing skills. He also served on the Agency's Inspector General's staff.

He teaches Intelligence Analysis and Writing for the FBI, the Treasury's Financial Crime Center (FinCEN) and has taught for members of the U.S. Intelligence Community including the Department of Homeland Security as well as the National Counter-Terrorism Center. He also teaches for the Royal Canadian Mounted Police, the Canadian Police College, the York Ontario Police, the Canada's Correctional Service, and the Singapore Police. Cariens also teaches workshops for the International Association of Law Enforcement Intelligence Agencies.

Cariens served as a member of the Ad-hoc Program Advisory Committee (PAC) for the development of the Bachelor of Applied Public Safety (BAPS), specialization in Crime and Intelligence Analysis at Seneca College, Toronto, Canada. He has taught at the University of Richmond's Osher Institute and was an adjunct professor at Virginia Commonwealth University's Homeland Security Department.

His textbook, *Critical Thinking Through Writing: Intelligence and Crime Analysis*, is the standard text for the Florida Department of Law Enforcement and is used nationwide. Cariens is a contributing author to the International Association of Law Enforcement Intelligence Agency's textbook, *Criminal Intelligence for the 21st Century*.

Cariens is a founder and director of the *Writers Guild of Virginia*.

Other Books By David Cariens

*A Question of Accountability: The Murder of Angela Dales**

*Virginia Tech: Make Sure It Doesn't Get Out**

Intelligence and Crime Terminology: A Glossary of Terms and Acronyms

The America We All Want: Protecting Your Community From Gun Violence

Critical Thinking Through Writing: Intelligence and Crime Analysis

Eight Steps to Writing Your Memoir

Effective Intelligence Briefing: A Guide for Intelligence Officers and Educators

Escaping Madness (a memoir)

*After taxes and expenses, all profits from those two books go to charities. Cariens takes no money for his work on behalf of shooting victims and their families.

Made in United States
Orlando, FL
13 August 2022

20967181R00088